15 MINUTE LOWFAT MEALS
A COOKBOOK FOR THE BUSY PERSON

by
Jayne Benkendorf

15 MINUTE LOWFAT MEALS
A COOKBOOK FOR THE BUSY PERSON

Library of Congress Cataloging-in-Publication Data
15 minute lowfat meals: a cookbook for the busy person
by Jayne Benkendorf
Includes index.
ISBN: 0-9651990-0-2

96-76210
CIP

15 MINUTE LOWFAT MEALS,
A COOKBOOK FOR THE BUSY PERSON
By Jayne Benkendorf
Copyright 1996 by Jayne Benkendorf

Printed in the United States of America by:
Morris Publishing
3212 E. Hwy. 30
Kearney, NE 68848

Book design by: DESIGNSMITH, INC. Oklahoma City, Oklahoma

DISCLAIMER:
It should be noted that in no way is any information contained
herein to be construed as a prescription or medical advice, or is
this information in any way to preclude the need or advice of a
health professional. In fact, it is recommended that should you
wish to change your diet because of any information contained
herein, you should first consult a health professional, especially if
you are currently taking medication and/or have a physical impair-
ment. All rights reserved. Furthermore, no information contained
herein may be used for the sale and/or promotion of any product or
service and is strictly prohibited by Jayne Benkendorf. If you do
not wish to be bound by the above, you may return this book for a
full refund to
MEALS IN MINUTES
P.O. Box 1828
Edmond, OK 73083-1828

TABLE OF CONTENTS

In all affairs it's a healthy thing now and then to hang a question mark on the things you have long taken for granted.

- Bertrand Russell

THE "FABULOUS 30", HIGH ENERGY FOODS

WHAT ARE THE "FABULOUS 30" FOODS?

The "Fabulous 30" foods are the best of the best. These are the foods that I use as the main ingredients in all of my meals. These are all very high energy foods. They're very rich in complex carbohydrates. These foods will not, and I stress will NOT, convert to fat easily. Research clearly indicates that any society, any group of people, or any person who dominates their diet with these type foods will NOT have weight problems. These foods are energy foods. They convert to energy easily - not to fat easily. These foods are to our body what high octane fuel is to our car. These are our high octane foods.

While most meals are planned around some kind of meat, the "Fabulous 30" concept is to plan meals around these high octane foods. When meats and dairy products dominate our diet, two problems occur. First these foods are not effective energy foods. For example, athletes have learned that these are the type foods that must be limited or eliminated prior to competition. Secondly, meats and dairy products can be high in fat, and foods high in fat convert to fat very easily. Please understand, I am not saying we should never eat meat and dairy products. Quite the contrary, as they supply valuable nutrients. All I'm saying is that they should not dominate our meals. In fact, I think our total intake of these type foods should be kept to 10% or less of our total food consumption.

Another common error we make in meal planning is with the use of highly processed foods - primarily the grains and the sugars. These type foods certainly dominate many of our meals. These foods are everywhere in our grocery stores, but we must not let these type foods dominate our meals. Why?

Highly processed foods have had most of their nutrients and fiber removed during processing. These foods leave our body still hungry. Have you ever eaten and eaten until you're stuffed, but you're still hungry? With these highly processed foods, we overeat because we are not giving our body what it needs. In addition, highly processed foods convert to fat more easily than their whole counterparts. For example, whole wheat bread is a very high energy food, whereas the highly processed white bread, in my opinion, does nothing more than add inches to the ole hips!

There are no highly processed foods in the "Fabulous 30" foods. In fact, the "Fabulous 30" are clearly at the other end of the scale - very high in nutrients, very high in fiber and very high in energy. With these foods you will find, as I have, you will get full before you get stuffed!

WHAT ABOUT THE "FABULOUS 30" RECIPES?

I have created complete meals which are dominated by one or more of the "Fabulous 30" foods. These are truly very high energy meals. These meals are put together using the basic concept that 50% to 60% of any meal should come from the high octane, energy foods; 30% to 40% should come from fresh or frozen fruits and vegetables; and not more that 10% from animal products and the fats.

I assure you, that if we adopt a lifestyle of eating whole foods in the proportions that are illustrated in these recipes, we will see our energy level increase, our attitude become more positive, and our weight problem begin to disappear.

These are the 30 recipes that I use the most. They are time tested. They work!

This is the incredible part. These meals take 15 minutes to get to the table!! I certainly don't like spending a lot of time in the kitchen, nor do I like washing a bunch of dirty pots and pans! I want good quality meals, but I don't want to take a lot of time fixing them. If you're like I am, you'll love these recipes!

WHY DIETS DON'T WORK

We starve ourselves, we limit calories, we count fat grams, we weigh our food, we measure our food, we use sugar substitutes, we use fat substitutes, we skip meals, we eat all sorts of crazy food combinations, and we keep on gaining weight - and we keep on going on diets. It's obvious, DIETS DON'T WORK!

I want to share this incident with you. A few years back a woman came to me in tears. She was literally crying. She said, "Jayne, I'm a failure. I don't know what I'm doing wrong." She told me, "10 years ago I was a little overweight, about 10 pounds. I went on a diet, and I lost the 10 pounds, but I gained it back plus some more. For 10 years I have done everything. I have been on every program around. I've tried them all." She was actually boo-hooing at this point. And she said, "Just look at me. I'm 60 pounds overweight! I don't have any energy, I hate myself, I'm depressed, I'm no fun to be around. What am I doing wrong?"

I got her calmed down, then I asked her one question. "Mary, during these last 10 years, have you gone hungry a lot?" I thought she was going to attack me. She jumped up, and said, "Are you crazy!

6

I'm hungry all the time! Don't you know anything about diets? You have to go hungry to lose weight." This lady was beside herself.

Well, I calmed her down again and told her about how I spent 20 years on those stupid diets - and if she thinks she did some silly things listen to some of mine. Do you know about the grapefruit diet that is supposed to 'melt away' the fat? Or how about this one; for 2 weeks I ate nothing but bananas and buttermilk! How stupid can you get! After 20 years of this I finally woke up and said to myself, "Hey, Jayne, something's wrong." So I began doing some soul searching and a lot of studying, and it all of a sudden dawned on me what I had been doing wrong - and it's so simple! I was starving myself into overweightness! And from then on I came to realize that if I were to get control of my body and achieve permanent weight control, I had to follow this key rule: Never Go Hungry! Etch that in your brain: NEVER GO HUNGRY!

Why is this so important? Well, let's just see what happens to our body when we go hungry. First of all, when we don't eat, we're telling our body to conserve energy. Our body has a natural built-in survival instinct. Let's say we got caught out in the desert with only one canteen of water. Would we drink it all at once, or would we ration it and make it last? Of course, we would make it last. This is exactly what our body does naturally when we restrict food. It holds onto our calories and rations them.

If we get in a pattern of not eating meals, or we restrict calories, our brain sends a message to the body to conserve energy. Now what does this mean? It means we don't burn calories. We hang onto them, oh boy, do we hang on. When this happens, our metabolism slows down and our energy decreases. Then, now get this, when we do eat a meal, our body won't burn these calories, at least not very well, because it remembers that it's not going to get anymore for quite a few hours, and the calories are stored as fat. That ugly stuff - fat. In a nutshell, this is why diets that restrict calories don't work. They never have and they never will!

Now, I'm not saying we won't lose weight if we restrict enough calories. We will. But the problem occurs when we start eating again - and we always do! We have trained our body to conserve energy, to hang onto our calories and to store these calories as fat. In other words, when we go on a diet, we're actually training ourselves to accumulate fat.

Studies are clearly telling us that when we eat the right foods, we can eat all we want, and we will not gain weight. As a well known promoter of the "Never Go Hungry" theory says, "Food does not make you fat. Fat makes you fat." This is so true. Think of this:

7

Why will a person gain weight when they eat 2,000 calories of the typical American diet (which is close to 40% fat); yet will lose weight when they eat 2,000 calories of predominately high energy food? The answer is simple: Energy foods do not convert to fat easily. They convert to energy. They keep our metabolism moving in high gear. They give us the energy to exercise. They're what give us pep; the get-up-and-go.

Do you know what the difference is between a couch potato with a negative attitude and an active, energetic person with a positive attitude? About 30 to 60 days of practicing the "Never Go Hungry" concepts and dominating the diet with the "Fabulous 30" foods.

If you're struggling with weight problems, I know what you're going through. I've been there. I also know the freedom we can enjoy without having this terrible yoke around our neck!

A WORD ABOUT EXERCISE

Regular exercise should become a natural part of our lives. However, when we do not eat energy foods, we simply do not have the energy to exert energy. We feel sluggish and develop the attitude of not really caring. This will change as you begin dominating your meals with the energy foods.

As your energy increases you need to add some form of exercise to your lifestyle. You may start by simply walking up a flight of stairs instead of using the elevator. Activity will actually begin to grow on you!

Two things happen to us when we exercise regularly. First, we keep our body's metabolism running in high gear. This is necessary for good health. It keeps our mind active, our organs functioning well, and it burns calories. Secondly, exercise builds muscle, and muscle tone makes our body look and move better. Years of dieting takes its toll on our muscles. Restricting calories causes our body to live off its own muscles, and the only way we can replace these muscles is through exercise.

I am often asked what kind of exercise is best. My only answer is this: The kind we enjoy the most. Generally, anything is better than what we have been doing. Personally, I enjoy dance aerobics; however, some people enjoy walking, jogging, stationary biking, Jazzercise, etc. You can join a club or you can participate at home.

In the future we'll be seeing more and more companies allowing time for their employees to exercise while at work. Evidence is very clear that periods of exercise during the day increase our productivity. However, the important thing for us is this: As our energy level increases, because of our improved eating habits, it will be easier for us to exercise - and we will want to!

GROUPING FOODS FOR WEIGHT CONTROL

If we eat the right assortment of healthful foods, we should never have to go hungry, never have to count calories, and we won't be afraid of those bathroom scales! When we group foods for weight control - and good health, we must ask two basic questions: Does this food convert to energy easily? Or, does this food convert to fat easily? By answering these two questions about all our foods, we can see that they fall into three basic food groups.

9

GROUP I (Fiber Rich, Energy Efficient Foods)

Foods in this group include all whole grains and whole grain products, all legumes and all complex carbohydrate vegetables. Foods in this group are good sources of fiber and are our very best energy foods. In other words, when we eat these foods, our body converts them to energy easily. In addition, and of great importance to us, these foods do not convert to fat easily.

These type foods should dominate our meals - 50% to 60% of our food intake should come from these foods. Athletes and individuals in special training programs will "jump" their intake of the energy foods up to 70% to 80%. The bottom line for us is this: Energy foods must dominate our food intake for optimum weight control and wellness.

This is what the "Fabulous 30" foods are all about. The "Fabulous 30" identifies our very best energy foods - the foods I personally eat for energy. Plan your meals around these foods, and you too will have permanent weight control, increased energy and a strong positive attitude - one that says, "Look out world, here I come!"

GROUP II (Fiber Rich, Neutral Energy Foods)

Foods in this group are the fruits and vegetables. They are just like the foods in Group I in that they are fiber rich and will not convert to fat easily. The difference is that these foods are not as high in energy.

From a health standpoint, we derive a tremendous amount of our nutrients from these foods, and they must be included in our diets. Without these foods, we would not realize all the benefits from the energy foods. We can fill our car with the very best high energy fuel available, but if our spark plugs aren't working right, we're wasting our money. Likewise, we can eat all the right energy foods, but if we do not include a generous supply of fruits and vegetables along with them, they won't be energized.

Remember, 50% to 60% of our food intake should come from the energy foods. Likewise, 30% to 40% of our food intake should come from fruits and vegetables. And how should our fruits and vegetables be eaten?

The very best is raw or lightly cooked or steamed. I do not think any canned fruit and most canned vegetables are good choices. (Canned tomatoes, legumes and some soups are exceptions.) I prefer fresh or frozen fruits and vegetables because they contain the most natural nutrients. Fruits and vegetables are fragile, and nutrients can be destroyed very easily. Overcooking is definitely not recommended.

GROUP III (Fiberless, Inefficient Energy Foods)

Foods in this group include all meats, dairy products, fats (butter, margarine, cooking oils, mayonnaise, salad dressings, etc.) and all highly processed foods. These foods contain very little or no fiber and do not convert to energy efficiently. The body just loves to store these type foods as fat! They convert very easily to fat in and on our body. It's little wonder we have so many weight problems in the United States because these foods dominate our diet. The key here is dominate. We need not eliminate these foods as they supply nutrients we need.

Lean meats and nonfat dairy products are our best choices, but they still should not amount to more than 10% of our total food intake. Most people find it difficult to reduce these foods to 10%, but this is because they're not replacing these foods with energy foods.

The whole concept of the "Never Go Hungry" eating lifestyle is just that: When we're hungry - eat! Just make sure it comes from foods in Groups I and II, not from foods in Group III.

A PARTIAL LISTING OF FOODS
WITHIN EACH FOOD GROUP:

GROUP I

WHOLE GRAINS
- Bagels
- Biscuits*
- Bread
- Cereal
- Corn
- Crackers*
- Grits
- Pancakes*
- Pasta
- Popcorn, raw
- Rice
- Tortillas, plain
- Waffles*
- Wheat Germ

LEGUMES
- Black Beans
- Blackeye Peas
- Garbanzos
- Green Peas
- Kidney Beans
- Lentils
- Lima Beans
- Navy Beans
- Pinto Beans
- Red Beans

POTATOES
- Sweet Potatoes
- White Potatoes

WINTER SQUASH
- Acorn
- Butternut
- Hubbard
- Spaghetti

GROUP II

VEGETABLES
- Asparagus
- Beets
- Broccoli
- Carrots
- Celery
- Cucumber
- Garlic
- Kale
- Leaf Lettuce
- Mushrooms
- Mustard Greens
- Okra
- Onions
- Parsley
- Sweet Peppers
- Spinach
- Summer Squash
- Crookneck
- Scallop
- Zucchini
- Tomatoes
- Turnips

FRUITS
- Apples
- Apricots
- Bananas
- Berries (all)
- Cantaloupe
- Grapefruit
- Grapes
- Nectarines
- Melons (all)
- Oranges
- Peaches
- Pears
- Pineapple
- Plums

GROUP III

MEATS
- Beef
- Chicken
- Fish
- Pork
- Turkey

DAIRY PRODUCTS
- Buttermilk
- Cheese
- Cottage Cheese
- Cream Cheese
- Frozen Yogurt
- Ice Cream
- Milk
- Sour Cream
- Yogurt

FATS
- Butter
- Cooking Oil
- Margarine
- Mayonnaise
- Salad Dressing

NUTS & SEEDS
- (Roasted in Oil)

EGGS

HIGHLY PROCESSED FOODS
- Candies
- Jellies
- Junk Foods
- Pastries
- White Breads
- White Flour

* Made with minimal fat

PLEASE NOTE:

You will notice that raw nuts and seeds are not included in any of these three food groups. They are an exception as they are an energy and a high fat food combined. My favorites are almonds, pecans and sunglower seeds. I use these often for flavor and crunch in many foods. They are very nutritious and give us energy, but since they are high in fat, they should be somewhat limited. Just remember, only the raw choices are acceptable.

SUMMARY:

You're holding in your hands, right now, the answer to the question, "What should I eat - to lose weight, stay trim and be healthy?" The *15 MINUTE LOWFAT MEALS* Cookbook that utilizes the "Fabulous 30" foods! These are the foods that dominate my meals and my snacks. I eat these foods when I'm hungry whether it's morning, noon or night - or somewhere in between. These foods do not make me fat. They will not make you fat. Only foods in Group III make us fat! WANT TO KEEP MOTIVATED? Then by all means, order "The Companion", my eight page newsletter. Let me visit with you ten times a year. Let me keep you motivated. Let me keep you informed about new products arriving on the market. Let me warn you about products to stay away from - products that look like they're healthful but are only imposters with hidden fat, highly processed ingredients, and additives and preservatives.

Let me keep you from getting bored by adding new recipes to these "Fabulous 30" recipes you already have. Let me be there when you need me. I stay motivated by writing "The Companion". You can stay motivated by reading "The Companion". Together we can have that energetic attitude which says, "Look out world, here I come!"

To order "The Companion" use the order form on pages 111 and 117.

13

THE "FABULOUS 30" FOODS

CEREAL   1

My Choice: Kellogg's Nutri-Grain

There are quite a few cold cereals that I recommend as good energy food, and Kellogg's Nutri-Grain is one of my top choices. There are two varieties of Nutri-Grain. One is Almond Raisin which is a wheat free cereal made with whole grain brown rice, whole grain corn, raisins and almonds. The other variety is Nutri-Grain Golden Wheat made of whole grain wheat and whole grain corn.

These cereals are excellent energy foods and make a great quick-to-fix breakfast. Never, and I mean never, add sugar to such a good food. I don't feel a sweetener is needed; however, if you disagree, simply add a little concentrated apple juice and this should do the trick. Adding fresh or frozen fruit such as strawberries, peaches, or a banana will add to the taste and nutrition.

Most cereals on our shelves are nothing more than fat or sugar factories, so we must be selective. Some other cereals that are good choices include: Grape Nuts, Kellogg's All Bran, Weetabix, and Raisin Bran by Post, Skinners & Kellogg's. There are many good cereals, these are just a few of them.

FOR SWEETENING: Instead of sugar or sugar substitutes, use apple juice concentrate. All brands of frozen apple juice concentrate are fine. If you can get juice from organically grown apples, that's the best. Concentrated apple juice is very sweet and is an excellent substitute for sugar, not only on cereal but most any-place where we would use sweetening. We get the sweetness of the juice as well as the nutrients it provides. Sugar gives us no nutrients.

I keep a pitcher of thawed apple juice concentrate in the refrigerator all the time. Give it a try. I think you'll like it.

17

2   PASTA

My Choice: Hodgson Mill

Pasta is a tremendous energy food but, just like other grain products, only if it is of the whole grain variety. I know we have become accustomed to associating pasta with weight gain, but this is because of the rich sauces that are added and because of the type pasta that is eaten.

White pasta is much like white bread; it will convert to fat easier than the whole grain variety, and it does not supply as much energy. Traditional white pasta is made from semolina flour. Semolina is durum wheat that has been stripped of its germ and bran. (There go the vitamins, minerals, fiber and energy!)

Whole grain pasta is altogether a different story. Energy, fiber and nutrients make the difference. The best pasta is made from whole durum wheat, a hard wheat that is grown primarily in the northern, central states. It is this whole wheat that gives good pasta its unique taste and texture.

Whole wheat pasta has a rich, nutty flavor and is much more filling and satisfying - because it has all of its nutrients and fiber. I prefer the Hodgson Mill brand of pasta. The shape of pasta makes no difference; however I generally prefer the macaroni (elbow) shape because it is so easy for children to eat. But I use them all from time to time.

WHAT TO PUT ON PASTA: How about a pasta sauce? One of my favorite brands is Healthy Choice. Healthy Choice is very low in fat, and all varieties have a wonderful flavor and consistency - they're thick, not runny!

Some other brands are very high in fat, and some contain cottonseed oil - an ingredient I believe we should avoid. You see, cotton is not a food crop, therefore the pesticides are not regulated for food.

If you want to add cooked meat to your sauce, that's fine. Just be sure that it is very lean, and use only a small amount. My favorites to add to pasta sauce are chopped clams and chopped oysters.

BROWN RICE 3

My Choice:
There are many good brands of brown rice.
I use Arrowhead Mills, Comet, Lundberg,
Mahatma, S&W and Uncle Ben's.

Notice, we're talking about brown rice - not the white rice that dominates our grocery shelves and is served in so many restaurants. White rice is not completely bad and does supply energy, but not as much as the more natural brown rice. I always recommend and use brown rice.

What about quick cooking brown rice?
My Choice: Uncle Ben's, Minute,
Arrowhead Mills, Success, and Gourmet Award
I was so excited when I first knew that quick cooking brown rice was available. It has been on the market for a few years, and quite a few manufacturers are carrying it.

Arrowhead Mills developed the technique that makes brown rice into a quick cooking rice. Regular brown rice is subjected to dry heat for a short period of time. The moisture that is inside each kernel turns to steam. When this steam is drawn out by the dry heat, it leaves tunnels inside the kernel. By this process, more surface area is created which enables the rice to be cooked in a shorter period of time.

Quick cooking brown rice contains the majority of the nutrients of the original brown rice, which makes it an excellent high energy, lowfat choice.

In my opinion, quick cooking brown rice does not have the flavor or texture of the long cooking rice, but I always keep it on hand for those times when I need rice really fast.

FOR FLAVORFUL RICE: Rice cooked in water doesn't have a lot of flavor. When I want more flavor, I cook rice in broth instead of water. If I want a poultry flavor, I use Swanson 1/3 Less Sodium Chicken Broth. When I want a beef flavor, I use Health Valley Beef Broth.

Many broths, and bouillons as well, contain MSG. These two products don't. (Swanson's regular chicken broth contains MSG, but not the 1/3 Less Sodium.)

4 WHOLE WHEAT BREAD

My Choice: 100% Whole Wheat by Earth Grains, Arnold, and Brownberry

When we're talking nutrition and energy, whole wheat bread has to be listed right at the top! Unfortunately, the real thing is sometimes hard to identify in the grocery store. Many, and I mean "a bunch", of the dark colored breads offered are only imposters with coloring added to make them look like whole wheat. These kinds are nothing more than white breads, and the only purpose I've figured out for them is putting extra pounds on the ole hips!

My favorite whole wheat bread choices are 100% Whole Wheat by Earth Grains, Arnold, and Brownberry.

WHAT TO PUT ON BREAD: If you're accustomed to putting a lot of butter on your bread, gradually decrease the amount you use until you no longer want butter. (This won't happen overnight, but it will happen.) Instead of butter, use a fruit jam made only with fruit and fruit juice. There are many good brands on the market. They include: Smucker's Simply Fruit, Polaner, R.W. Knudsen, Sorrell Ridge, and Poiret.

Also, try some apple butter on whole wheat toast. The brands I use are Smucker's Simply Fruit Apple Butter, L&A, and R.W. Knudsen.

BEANS (Legumes) 5

My Choice: Kidney Beans by S&W, Black Beans by Ranch Style, and Chili Hot Beans by Bush's

I eat a lot of beans. The beans I'm talking about are legumes; pintos, blackeye peas, garbanzos, kidneys, lentils, limas, etc. These beans are very low in fat (it's practically nonexistent) and are very high in energy.

I guess what I like most about beans, beside their taste, is that they can be used in so many different ways; in chili, in vegetable salads, pasta salads, in soups & stews, on potatoes, to name a few.

I will cook a pot of beans from "scratch", but I always keep canned beans in my pantry because they are so handy. I have three favorite kinds of canned beans; Chili Hot Beans by Bush's, Kidney Beans by S&W, and Black Beans by Ranch Style.

A bit about each of these wonderful legumes:

KIDNEY BEANS (S&W)

There are many brands of kidney beans on the market, but very few are free of ethylenediamine tetra-acetic acid (EDTA). EDTA is used to attract metal.

EDTA in food products attracts metals that are vital to good health: calcium, iron, zinc, magnesium, copper and others. Because of this mineral loss, many health professionals recommend that pregnant and nursing women avoid foods with EDTA. I'm certainly not pregnant or nursing, but I don't want robbed of calcium, or any of the other valuable nutrients.

One of my favorite brands of kidney beans is S&W. S&W also has a 50% Less Salt variety. This is much lower in sodium than the regular variety, but it still is a bit high in sodium. With either variety, if you need to watch your sodium intake, rinse the beans well with running water.

21

BLACK BEANS (Ranch Style)

Black Beans by Ranch Style is one of my favorite brands. Did you know that black beans are great added to a vegetable salad? Since they're high in sodium, you may want to rinse them with running water, then add them to your greens and chopped vegetables.

Use them in all sorts of Mexican dishes. A fun lunch I like to make is a burrito sort of thing. Just do this:

To a corn tortilla, add some fresh spinach leaves; top with a couple tablespoons of rinsed black beans, top those with chopped tomatoes and green onions. If you'd like, sprinkle a little shredded low moisture, part skim mozzarella cheese on the very top. Now, microwave for about 30 seconds or so.

Add some salsa, if you'd like some extra zip. (I like Pace Picante Sauce.) This is so quick to fix, is very attractive and very tasty.

Beans are relatively inexpensive, but if food were priced based on the energy it supplied, beans would be that higher priced, super unleaded fuel!

CHILI HOT BEANS (BUSH'S)

Chili Hot Beans, like all legumes are packed with energy and are extremely low in fat - just a tiny trace. Since the Mexican flavor is popular with so many people, including me, this is a great bean to use for that unique Mexican taste.

I like to use Bush's Chili Hot Beans when I make chili, and I also use them to top a baked potato. See the recipes on pages 79, 89, and 93.

FOR EXTRA FLAVOR: If you like the Mexican flavor, add salsa or picante sauce to your beans. My favorite brand is Pace. If you want just a bit of the Mexican flavor, use the "mild" variety. If you want your tongue on fire, use "hot".

OATMEAL 6

My Choice: Quaker Old Fashioned

This may be one of our very best grain choices. When we talk about health, fiber, ease of digestion and high energy, we really have a winner here. This is my husband's favorite cereal, but you ought to see the way he eats it. To start with, he only cooks it for about 15 seconds in boiling water. (That's right, he cooks it. He won't let me prepare it.) After it's cooked, he adds concentrated apple juice for sweetener, then he adds a heaping tablespoon of wheat germ and a handfull of raisins. Since he doesn't want milk to ruin a good thing, he adds water.

I'll have to admit, you can't put much more energy in a cereal bowl, and it tastes great. The fruit taste from the apple juice concentrate and the raisins really sets it off. If you're not eating oatmeal now, I encourage you to rediscover this exceptional high energy and almost no-fat food. If you don't like it mushy, don't let it cook so long.

I know one person who eats it like cold cereal. She just adds milk. And oatmeal isn't just for breakfast anymore. Eat it like a snack.

FOR SWEETENING: Use apple juice concentrate (see page 17).

FOR CRUNCH & FLAVOR: Try Kretschmer Wheat Germ. Are you one of the many people who has never tried wheat germ? If so, you're not alone. Many people have never eaten wheat germ. It is very tasty as well as nutritious. It has a wonderful nutty flavor, and this is why I like to serve it on top of yogurt - either the frozen or refrigerated varieties. Wheat germ is an excellent source of protein, fiber, B vitamins, iron, selenium and vitamin E. Two tablespoons of wheat germ supply us with half the vitamin E the USRDA says we need in a day. I always add wheat germ to muffins, pancakes, waffles, biscuits, cookies, oatmeal etc. I encourage you to add wheat germ to your grocery list. Just refrigerate it after it has been opened. Wheat germ is not lowfat. It is 27% fat, which is under the 30% recommended by many health organizations, but in my books 27% is high. But because a small amount of wheat germ is such a powerhouse of nutrients and energy, it is important to include it in our foods.

7   REFRIED BEANS

My Choice: Rosarita, No Fat

Many people think refried beans are high in fat, and they can be. It's usually in restaurants where we find high fat refried beans because the chef adds extra fat to the canned beans. Refried beans, right out of the can, usually are not high in fat. Rosarita, No Fat Refried Beans is truly a fat free, high energy food.

The biggest complaint I hear about beans is that they cause gas. It's true they do - if you're not accustomed to eating them. Eating beans is like everything else - start gradually. Eat only a tablespoon or two at a time, then gradually increase the amount until you can eat all you want. If you eat beans only a few times a year, you will have gas. It's guaranteed!

Enjoy refried beans. Use them in dips, as a side dish, for making burritos, chalupas, soft tacos and much more.

WHAT TO USE WITH REFRIED BEANS: Picante sauce! I always mix Pace "Hot" Picante Sauce in my refried beans. (I like really hot Mexican food!) Then I dip in some corn tortilla chips - see page 38 and have a feast!

POTATO (Irish)   8

If I were forced to rank foods for energy, I believe the potato would go at the top of the list. What's really ironic is that nearly all my life (the years I had a weight problem) the potato was one food I was told I sure couldn't eat. Everyone knew that potatoes made us fat! How wrong we were. I'll guarantee you, we can eat all the baked potatoes we want, everyday, and we will not gain weight. We just need to be very careful what we put on potatoes. (Butter and sour cream are out, but let's look at what we can use; fresh chives, green onions, salsa, beans, soups, nonfat yogurt, fat free cottage cheese and all sorts of spices. Try the recipes on pages 53, 71, and 89.)

Other high fat potato choices we need to avoid include fried potatoes, potato chips and all the creative versions of fried potatoes such as the "tots" etc.

Did you know that you can eat 298 baked potatoes and get less fat than in one 3 1/2 ounce prime rib!! Care to guess which choice would give us the most energy?

POTATO TOPPERS: If you're accustomed to eating butter and sour cream on your potato, use Butter Buds or Molly McButter.

It is difficult for me to believe that these products do not contain additives or preservatives. But they are high in sodium.

9   SWEET POTATO

Sweet potatoes are absolutely packed with energy and fiber, and fat is nonexistent - unless we add it. Sweet potatoes come in different colors, anywhere from white to orange to a purplish red. The orange colored varieties are highest in beta carotene, a powerful antioxidant.

American yams and sweet potatoes have the same food value, but not so for tropical yams. Tropical yams have no beta carotene. Most all yams we see in our supermarkets are American yams. If you're not sure which kind your store has, ask the produce person if the yams are American.

There is no comparison between an oven-baked sweet potato, or yam, and one that is microwave-baked. The oven-baked is so moist and sweet, and I can assure you that you will not need to add anything to it, only a little pepper and salt if you'd like.

Don't have time to bake sweet potatoes in the oven? Well, bake a big batch on the weekend, eat what you want when they're baked, then after the leftovers are cool, put them in a container and refrigerate. During the week when you want a sweet potato, just slice or chunk it into a pot, add a bit of water and heat till warm.

When these power packed foods are in season, enjoy them often.

SWEET POTATO TOPPERS: If you just "have" to add butter to your sweet potato, use either Butter Buds or Molly McButter.

If you like candied sweet potatoes, use apple juice concentrate in place of the usual sweetener. (Add some raisins, too.)

WINTER SQUASH   **10**

What is winter squash? Winter squashes are the ones that take a long time to cook - because they are complex carbohydrates. They are filled with energy and fiber and have no fat. The winter squashes include butternut, hubbard, spaghetti and acorn. (Pumpkin belongs to this family as well.)

Just so you will know, summer squashes include zucchini, scallop and yellow crookneck. These squashes cook very quickly because they are simple carbohydrate vegetables, but are not energy packed like the winter squashes; however, they contain valuable vitamins and minerals which we need.

Winter squashes are also good sources of beta carotene, but nothing like sweet potatoes, American yams or pumpkin.

I like to cut acorn squashes in half, scoop out the seeds, invert on a plate and microwave till done. These are very tasty - and quick to fix. Add just a little salt and pepper, and you have a scrumptious, high energy food.

SEASONINGS: If you like the buttery taste, use Butter Buds or Molly McButter along with a bit of salt and pepper.

Try eating vegetables plain to get the "real" taste of the food. If this doesn't turn your taste buds on, use seasonings.

11   CORN

Corn is one of those wonderful foods that I was told years ago to stay away from if I wanted to lose weight. How wrong "diets" were back then! Corn is a high energy, lowfat, complex carbohydrate that is certainly on my "eat list" now.

We can buy fresh corn, frozen corn and canned corn. However, canned corn is not the best choice.

Corn is a grain, and as such, makes a perfect complete protein combination with legumes. This is why beans and corn bread, as well as refried beans and tortilla chips, make wonderful meals.

Add corn to your shopping list, and add it to soups and stews and to vegetable salads - or eat it on the cob. (Just don't add butter - enjoy the true taste of the corn.) If you are accustomed to eating corn with butter, gradually cut down on the amount you use until you can enjoy corn without the taste of fat.

Want to try something a little different? If you have the opportunity, eat just-picked-corn raw. If you have never tried it, don't turn up your nose. It is fantastic! It is good raw only when you pick it right off the stalk.

SEASONINGS: As you can tell, I like my veggies plain - without seasonings. But if you like the buttery taste, use Molly McButter or Butter Buds.

There are some spices that are wonderful combinations of herbs, with no salt. Mrs. Dash has a wide variety as does Natural Blend & Parsley Patch. Experiment and see which you like best.

PEAS 12

This is another of those wonderful foods that I was told I couldn't eat if I wanted to lose weight. I get angry when I think of all the foods I did without for years because I was always on a "diet". I didn't eat bread, potatoes, corn or peas. This is absolutely ridiculous! I'll tell you what, I'm making up for lost time and enjoying every minute of it. The greatest thing is that I never think about my weight now. I am trim and healthy, and I'm enjoying life, and food - the right kinds.

Peas are complex carbohydrates, which means they are high energy, lowfat foods. They are also legumes, thus they are an excellent protein combination with grains including corn. See the recipe on page 61.

Peas are great to add to soups, stews, casseroles, pasta salads and vegetable salads. Fresh or frozen are the best choices. Use them every chance you get.

SEASONINGS: For the buttery taste, use Molly McButter or Butter Buds.

SALAD DRESSING: Salad dressings can be a real problem because so many are high in fat or sugar.

The dressings I use for vegetable salads and pasta salads are Good Seasons Fat Free Dressings: Italian, Honey Mustard, Zesty Herb & Creamy Italian. These dressings truly are fat free, but they are very high in sodium. For lower sodium, either dilute the dressing with water or use a small amount of dressing.

For a creamy dressing, mix plain, nonfat yogurt into the dressing. (I always add a minced garlic clove to all salad dressings.)

13   CORN MEAL & CORN BREAD MIX

My Choice: Arrowhead Mills, Hodgson Mill

For those of us who like to make our own corn bread and corn meal muffins from "scratch", I recommend Arrowhead Mills and Hodgson Mill corn meal. Both are made of 100% yellow corn meal with nothing taken out or nothing added.

Degerminated corn meal, such as Quaker Corn Meal, has to be enriched to put back into the product some of what has been taken out. It is enriched only with these nutrients: niacin, iron, thiamine & riboflavin. Obviously, other nutrients are destroyed, but only these four are replaced.

Just a note: Since bugs know a good thing when they smell it, if you don't plan using the whole grain corn meal right away, store it in the refrigerator or freezer. By contrast, degerminated corn meal will keep for years at room temperature. The life is taken out of it!

What about corn bread mix?
My Choice: Arrowhead Mills Corn Bread Mix

Many of us don't want to take the time to make corn bread from "scratch". This is why I keep Arrowhead Mills Corn Bread Mix on hand - it's so quick and easy. Corn bread is a very high energy, lowfat food - if we don't add butter, that is.

Most corn bread mixes are made with degerminated cornmeal - but not these. Because whole corn meal mix will not set on the shelf forever, keep it in the regrigerator or freezer.

Keep corn bread mix on hand to fix with your next pot of beans, or soup, or to have with most any meal. Your family will praise you!

WHAT TO PUT ON CORNBREAD: As you probably suspect, I don't put butter on my corn bread. But years ago I used a lot of butter. I gradually cut down the amount until now, I don't use any. I prefer the taste of the corn bread by itself.

If you use butter, I suggest that you gradually cut down. You might try using apple butter or an all fruit jam in place of the butter. For the brands to use, see page 20.

30

BULGUR - TABOLI WHEAT 14

My Choice: Steakhouse

There are various spellings for taboli, as well as bulgur; tabbouleh and bulghur are a couple. Taboli salad is made of bulgur. Bulgur is cracked wheat that has been partially cooked and then toasted. Bulgur cooks in a very short time, and it will also soften simply by letting it set in water.

Because the wheat berries have both the bran and germ, bulgur is a powerhouse when it comes to nutrients, fiber and energy.

There are many brands of bulgur on the market. Most supermarkets display their bulgur in the produce department. If you don't find it, just ask.

Most all taboli salad is very high in fat, but not my recipe. Give it a try and see what you think. I hope you enjoy it as much as my family does. See recipe on page 73.

BARLEY 15

My Choice: Quaker

Barley is a grain that we don't see used often. I don't know why this is. Maybe after you give it a try, you will find it on your table more often.

Whole barley has an indigestible outer hull. Pearled barley has this outer hull removed to reduce the cooking time. Quick pearled barley cooks even faster because it has been flattened by rollers. In fact, it resembles whole, rolled oats. It takes only 10 minutes to cook the quick variety.

Barley has the same high energy and the almost no fat characterictics of the other grains, and it offers a new taste. Try the recipe on page 75, and see what you think.

16 WHOLE WHEAT FLOUR

My Choice: Arrowhead Mills, Gold Medal, Hodgson Mill and Pillsbury

WHOLE WHEAT PASTRY FLOUR

My Choice: Arrowhead Mills

Let's talk about both of these fantastic products together since they are so similar. The only difference between them is, whole wheat pastry flour is made from soft wheat and is ground for a fine-textured finished product, while regular whole wheat flour is made from hard wheat. Both are made by using the entire whole wheat berry. This includes the outside bran layer and the germ, as well as the starchy endosperm.

Hard wheat is high in gluten - this is the protein that is elastic and responds to yeast in bread baking. Gluten is what causes light, airy loaves of bread. If we use regular whole wheat flour in unyeasted baked goods such as biscuits, pancakes, muffins, cookies, etc., they will be somewhat dense and heavy. Many people like this kind of texture. If you like yours lighter, just use whole wheat pastry flour.

Whole wheat pastry flour, made from soft wheat, is lower in gluten. Just remember, if you want a light texture in foods that do not require yeast, use whole wheat pastry flour. But for foods with yeast, use regular whole wheat flour.

Whether we use regular whole wheat or whole wheat pastry flour, both are very high energy, lowfat foods filled with vitamins, minerals and fiber. In all your baking, use either of these. As soon as you finish your bleached or unbleached stuff, stock your pantry with whole wheat. You'll feel great about giving your family these high quality foods.

ADD CRUNCH TO BAKED GOODS WITH: Sunflower kernels. Sunflower kernels, or nuts, are absolutely wonderful. These little morsels are packed with vitamins, minerals, fiber and protein. You may be picturing the sunflower kernels that are at the end of salad bars. I'm not talking about these! These have been fried in fat, are coated with salt, and have MSG!

UGH! In fact, many of the sunflower kernels on our grocery shelves are the very same. But there are some that are dry roasted or raw. Raw is the best choice as these kernels have more nutrients than the dry roasted. Unfortunately many supermarkets do not carry raw kernels, only the dry roasted. However, most all health food stores carry raw sunflower kernels. If you are not fortunate enough to have a grocery store that carries raw kernels, look for a health food store, and stock up on these little gems. I keep a jar of kernels handy in the refrigerator and freeze the rest until I'm ready to use them.

Sunflower kernels are also very high in fat. In fact, they're 78% fat. Because they are so nutritious and packed with energy, we should eat them, but not go overboard. I add them to salads, pancakes, waffles, biscuits, muffins, cookies, on top of yogurt, etc.

17 MUFFIN MIXES

My Choice: Arrowhead Mills and Hodgson Mill

I like to make muffins from "scratch", but there are occasions when I just don't want to take the time, so I'll grab a box of muffin mix.

There are a few brands of good, high energy, lowfat muffins on the market. Among them are; Arrowhead Mills, Hodgson Mill and Hain. I use either Arrowhead Mills or Hodgson Mill then I "doctor it up" by adding raisins, wheat germ and chopped nuts or seeds.

So many muffins and snack-cake type snacks are made with energy and nutrient deficient white flour with lots of fat and highly processed sugar. These foods rob us of energy and add fat to the waistline.

It is so easy to whip up a batch of high energy, lowfat muffins from a mix. If you have children, let them help you make the muffins. They will have fun doing it, and they will enjoy the muffins more when they have helped make them. (See if you can get them to help clean up the mess, too!)

"DOCTOR THEM UP" WITH: Sliced almonds.

Do you like nuts but won't eat them because they are so high in fat? It is true, nuts are high in fat. But the good news is that we must have some fat in our diet. In fact there is one fat that we must eat for good health. It is called linoleic acid. Doesn't sound like a fat, does it? It is, and it is absolutely essential that we get it daily. The only place we can get linoleic acid is from plant foods, and nuts and seeds are the best sources.

As I said, nuts are high in fat. Almonds are 74% fat. They are also great sources of bone-building nutrients (calcium & magnesium), iron, zinc, fiber, and they contain many other valuable nutrients.

When buying any nuts or seeds, buy only the raw varieties. Many packaged nuts are toasted in oil, and some even have seasonings with additives and preservatives.

It is important to include nuts and seeds in our diet, we just don't want to go overboard.

BISCUIT MIX 18

My Choice: Arrowhead Mills

This is another super, high energy, lowfat mix for the busy person. I don't know anyone who doesn't like biscuits, but unless you really like to cook and have the time, you're not going to make biscuits from "scratch".

(You know those biscuits we see in the refrigerated section of our stores? I don't even consider these food! They are made with highly processed flour and are absolutely loaded with additives and preservatives.)

I use Arrowhead Mills Multi Grain Biscuit Mix. The recipe on the package says to use 1/4 cup oil, but I use only 2 TB oil and add 2 TB water.

Did you know that you can really give some "zip" to your biscuits by adding spices? Try Italian seasoning or a bit of dill or celery seed, or chopped onion. Be creative.

WHAT TO PUT ON A BISCUIT: I like my biscuits without anything added to them, but if you like something sweet, use an all-fruit jam such as Smucker's Simply Fruit, or any of the other brands listed on page 20. Try to do without adding butter.

19 PANCAKE & WAFFLE MIXES

My Choice: Arrowhead Mills

Pancake and waffle mixes are so convenient for those hearty weekend breakfasts. But who's to say we should eat pancakes only for breakfast anyway! Have them anytime. If you don't want to make yours from "scratch", just use a mix that is made with whole grains such as Arrowhead Mills Multi Grain. It contains whole wheat, whole corn, brown rice and whole rye flours.

Pancakes or waffles made from a mix like this are just "bustin" with energy, and they're lowfat. I always add a little extra nutrition, and crunch, to my pancakes. I throw in about 1/4 cup raw sunflower kernels, sliced almonds, or chopped pecans to a batch of pancakes or waffles.

I like to make extra waffles to freeze, so all I have to do is put them in the toaster for a quick breakfast during the week.

If you prefer syrup, use the real stuff. The ones I use are Old Colony and Cary's Real Maple Syrup. Only real maple syrup is acceptable. All others are imposters made from very highly processed sugars with additives and preservatives.

I remember one Saturday morning walking into a restaurant that featured whole grain foods. In clear view was this gentleman sitting at a table eating the largest stack of pancakes I had ever seen. They looked 12 inches across and were stacked 4 inches high! Not realizing, I must have stopped and stared at him, because he looked up and said, "What's the matter, lady? Haven't you ever seen someone eat pancakes?" My response was, "Yes, but never so many. How do you keep from getting fat?" Do you know what he said? "If you eat the right foods, you'll never get fat, regardless of how much you eat."

That was probably ten years ago that this happened, and it didn't take me long to figure out what he was talking about. Since then, I have sat down to some pretty big meals myself, and it sure feels good knowing that I won't walk away a fatter person.

WHAT TO PUT ON TOP: Try heated apple juice concentrate. This is very sweet, and nutritious as well. Or try any of the all-fruit jams such as Simply Fruit by Smuckers. These have no refined sugars in them.

BOXED DINNERS 20

My Choice: Pritikin

Normally I don't have anything good to say about boxed dinners, but Pritikin Dinners are excellent. They have two varieties; Oriental Dinner and Mexican Dinner. To make these a complete meal just add a can of beans or a small amount of chicken, turkey or shrimp. I always add steamed vegetables on the side, such as broccoli, cabbage, cauliflower, etc.

These Pritikin Dinners are made with high energy brown rice and they're very low in fat. I keep Pritikin Dinners in my pantry for those days when I'm especially lazy.

Nearly every supermarket carries Pritikin products. If yours doesn't have these dinners, ask for them.

CANNED SOUPS 21
With whole grains, beans, or potatoes

My Choice: Health Valley

There are some wonderful, hearty, high energy, fat free, canned soups by Health Valley on our grocery shelves. All the grains used in Health Valley canned soups are whole grains - the rice is brown rice, and the noodles are made with whole wheat. No highly processed grains in these soups, and there's no fat! Can't beat a deal like this!

I like to keep these soups on hand for a really quick meal when I don't want to take the time to cook. One of my favorite soups is Real Italian Minestrone.

Unfortunately most of the soups on our grocery shelves wouldn't impress Grandma! Most have highly processed ingredients with fat and lots of sodium added - but not these canned soups by Health Valley. Grandma would be proud!

22 CORN TORTILLAS & TORTILLA CHIPS

My Choice: Our House, Del Sol, Jimenez, and Orbit

Soft corn tortillas are one of my favorite foods, and it seems that most everyone enjoys corn tortillas. I like to warm them in the microwave, roll them up, then dip them in salsa. By the way, when you eat in a Mexican restaurant, ask for soft corn tortillas to dip in your salsa instead of the fried variety that comes at the start of every meal. (Just be sure the cook hasn't added fat to the soft tortilla!)

At home I use corn tortillas to make soft tacos, chalupas, burritos, enchiladas, etc. Be creative, and enjoy this wonderful, high energy, lowfat food.

JUST A NOTE: There are many brands of locally produced tortillas. Choose those made only of corn, water and lime. (Since tortillas are treated with lime, they're a good source of absorbable calcium.)

What about the tortilla chips?
My Choice: Guiltless Gourmet
Guiltless Gourmet makes wonderful high energy, lowfat, great tasting chips.

I must quote to you from the bag. "Guiltless Gourmet chips are baked, not fried, and contain only four ingredients - corn, water, lime and salt in the salted variety. Therefore, when you eat a Guiltless Gourmet chip, you get the real, fresh, crunchy taste of corn, not a big dollop of preservative filled grease on top of a soaked and saturated glob of corn too battered to even cry out for help." I couldn't have said it better!!

Read on: "When you pick up (Guiltless Gourmet chips), you're holding a bag of honest corn tortilla chips. A bag of fried chips owes up to 35% of its weight to oil and over 50% of its calories to fat. Yuk! That's not what you want to get in return for your hard-earned cash. In a 7-ounce bag of Guiltless Gourmet chips, you usually get as many chips as you will find in a 10-ounce bag of the other guys' chips, because the weight is not taken up by oil."

These chips are one of my favorite snacks. Wonderful flavor and crunch!

FOLLOWING ARE EIGHT OF MY FAVORITE READY-MADE SNACK FOODS. MOST SNACK FOODS ARE A DISASTER FOR WEIGHT CONTROL, BUT NOT THESE EIGHT CHOICES. THEY ARE ALL HIGH ENERGY, LOWFAT AND NUTRITIOUS. AND THEY TASTE GOOD TOO!

CRACKERS 23

My Choice: Health Valley, RYVITA, Kavli, Finn Crisp

Crackers can be a terrible choice if we do not know what we're looking for; however, if crackers are made with whole grains with no fat or additives or preservatives, they are an excellent energy food. There are four brands that I really enjoy and think are great. They are: Health Valley, RYVITA, Kavli and Finn Crisp. All of these crackers are great for snacks and with soup or salads. They are also easy to keep with you in the car or slip into your desk at work.

WHAT TO SPREAD ON A CRACKER: Do you like cream cheese on a cracker? "Real" cream cheese is very high in fat. In fact, it is higher in fat than any other cheese. But you can make your own cream cheese that is fat free and tastes wonderful.

Put a carton of plain, nonfat yogurt in a small-holed colander. Place it over a bowl and let set in the refrigerator for a couple days - until all the excess liquid drains off. (If you stir the yogurt ever so often, it will drain faster.)

Now you have a semi-solid yogurt that tastes remarkably like cream cheese - but without the fat!

24 POPCORN

My Choice: Raw kernels only, all brands

When we think about it, popcorn has to be one of the most original and unique foods available. Popcorn has to rate as the king of all snack foods. I don't feel there is a week that goes by that I don't fix a batch or two of popcorn. It is great finger food - very rich in energy and very low in fat.

We Americans, however, have tried to ruin a high energy food. We have added fat, fat, fat in the form of cooking oil and butter (sometimes cheese) and lots of salt until a good, healthful food has become a health hazard! Folks, this just won't work. We need to rediscover the "real" taste of popcorn. The only, and I emphasize "only", way popcorn should be eaten is plain with nothing added. It took me about two weeks to get used to the taste of real popcorn, and now just the thought of the buttered, greasy stuff turns my stomach!

25 BREADSTICKS

My Choice: Whole wheat by Gardetto's, Angonoa's, Oroweat

Do you like something crunchy for an afternoon snack? Do you like crackers with your soup or salad? Then give these whole wheat breadsticks a try. These are not only crunchy, they are satisfying and packed with energy and fiber.

Most breadsticks are made with that nutrient and energy deficient white flour and have additives and preservatives - but not these.

One thing about breadsticks, they're so small they can easily be tucked in a purse or briefcase and go right with you for a quick snack when the hungries hit. Also, take them with you to eat with soup or a salad.

PRETZELS 26

My Choice: Whole wheat by Barbara's or Wege

Pretzels make great snacks. Snacks can be our downfall, or they can be a great pick-me-up. Most snacks are swimming in fat, are made with highly processed flour and sugar, and contain additives and preservatives. But these pretzels, by either Barbara's or Wege, are made with whole wheat - organic whole wheat at that - so they are satisfying, energy filled, and they are fat free. They also satisfy that urge to "crunch".

I keep a few in a zip lock bag and take with me when I'm on the road - in a car or plane.

As always, if your favorite store doesn't have these, they can get them.

A TASTE TREAT: Dip pretzels in plain, nonfat yogurt. I certainly think this tastes good. Give it a try.

FOOD FOR THOUGHT

Always remember, when I use the expression, "Never Go Hungry," I mean it. When we're hungry, this means our motor is running and our fuel tank is on "E". This says we'd better look for some quality fuel, and things like these quality snacks are premium fuel that give us energy. A snack can pick us up and give us energy, or it can pull us down and add the pounds. It's our choice!

27 FRUIT BARS

My Choice: Health Valley

There are some wonderful fruit bars by Health Valley. The varieties are Apricot, Date, Raisin & Apple. These bars are made with organic whole grains, fruits and fruit juices. They make a truly nutritious breakfast or snack. They're packed with vitamins, minerals, fiber, and complex carbohydrates. They're loaded with energy, and they're Fat Free. Can't beat a snack like this!

These bars are individually wrapped which makes them easy to toss in a lunch bag or in a briefcase. Add these to your shopping list for those times when you're rushed for breakfast, or for a pick-me-up in the afternoon.

28 BANANA

Generally, fruits and vegetables are not considered complex carbohydrates (high energy foods). But I don't care what the textbooks say, in my opinion, the banana is an exception and is a good energy food. It works that way for me and many others. I always have bananas available and eat them mainly as a snack when I feel a hunger pang or need a little pick-me-up. I also add them to cereal and use them in a fruit salad. They are also an excellent snack for children - and children just love them.

Be creative with bananas, and give this a try. Get some slightly overripe bananas, peel them and put them separately in Baggies, then freeze. Now, when the children come in for a snack, offer them one of these frozen guys. I'll guarantee you, they'll love them. They eat just like a popsicle - but oh so much better!

COOKIES 29

My Choice: Health Valley

Now I'm sure you will think I've lost my marbles because everyone knows that if anything will put on the pounds it's cookies. And 99% of the time, cookies are a bad choice because most are made with highly processed flour and sugars. But here we have something unique. Just look at the ingredient list:

Organic 100% whole wheat
Organic oats
All natural pineapple, pear and apple juice

And each cookie has 3 grams of fiber. This is fantastic!

We can definitely upgrade the quality of our snacks and our childrens' snacks with cookies like these. Health Valley offers many varieties of Fat Free Cookies. These cookies not only are great snacks, they are great for breakfast on those mornings when we, or the kids, are running behind. Some of these cookies with a glass of orange juice make a very good breakfast. (Your kids will look at you in amazement when you tell them to have some cookies for breakfast!)

GRANOLA BARS 30

My Choice: Health Valley

Health Valley makes several varieties of high energy, Fat Free, Granola Bars. Each variety is very tasty, and they're made with whole grains only. Each bar is individually wrapped and easy to take to work or school.

I hear so many people say they don't have time for breakfast. With these Granola Bars, there's nothing to do - just eat and then run - or eat while on the run!

THE
"FABULOUS 30" RECIPES

This recipe is for all the Mexican food lovers out there - and this includes me. The problem we have with this tasty food is: How can we make it taste good without the fat?

ARROZ CON POLLO   1
Makes 6 servings

3/4 pound boneless, skinless chicken breast,
     cut into thin strips
1/2 tsp. cumin
1/2 tsp. chili powder
2 tsp. sunflower oil
1 small onion, chopped
1 garlic clove, minced
1 can (14 1/2 oz) tomatoes
1/3 cup picante sauce *(Pace)*
1 cup hot water
2 cups QUICK COOKING BROWN RICE *(Uncle Ben's)*
1 can (8 oz) KIDNEY BEANS, drained *(S&W)*

Heat oil in skillet; sprinkle chicken with cumin & chili powder; sauté chicken 2 to 3 minutes. Add onion & garlic; stir. Add tomatoes, water & picante sauce; heat to boiling. Add rice; reduce heat; cover & simmer 5 minutes. Stir in beans. Let set, covered, 3 minutes for all liquid to absorb.

Add a steamed vegetable such as broccoli or cauliflower, or make a salad. If you use salad dressing, use a very small amount.

Personally, I like my Mexican food fairly spicy, so I use a bit more chili powder, and cumin as well. Of course, you can use a mild or hot picante sauce to change the temperature of this dish.

You can purchase the chicken already skinned, boned and cut into thin strips. This is more expensive than preparing your own, but it definitely saves time.

If you are concerned about your sodium intake, purchase no-salt tomatoes and rinse the kidney beans. The only thing left that contains sodium is the picante sauce.

This is one of my family's favorite meals. I hope yours likes it too.

NOTES

ARROZ CON POLLO

Per Serving:

Calories: 285   *Sodium: 335 mg*

Fat: 5 g   *Fiber: 4 g*

Do you like pizza? Who doesn't! Why not have a pizza sandwich? Pack one (or two) in your, or your child's, lunch.

Make your shopping list now for this great tasting meal. This sandwich fills you up so you won't be hungry a couple hours after eating. Most everyone will like this taste because it has a mild pizza flavor - but without all the fat of pizza.

PIZZA SANDWICH 2
Makes 1 serving

2 slices WHOLE WHEAT BREAD
1/4 cup shredded low moisture, part skim
    mozzarella cheese
2 TB spaghetti sauce (*Healthy Choice*)

Toast the bread; sprinkle a thin layer of shredded mozzarella cheese on one slice. Drop spaghetti sauce on the cheese; top with another thin layer of cheese; then add the second piece of toast. Put in a Baggie, and now all you have to do is wait for lunch!

Also eat fresh veggies; carrot sticks, cauliflower, green or red pepper, etc. Also have a pear or an apple and a couple of cookies. Health Valley Fat Free cookies are great.

FOOD FOR THOUGHT
All recipes in *15 MINUTE LOWFAT MEALS* are planned around complex carbohydrates (energy foods), not around meat as most American meals are. I know that it is difficult to change our thought process to: "What kind of complex carbohydrate will I fix for dinner?" instead of "What kind of meat am I going to have for dinner?" But we need to think in terms of planning the entire meal around such foods as potatoes, sweet potatoes, brown rice, whole wheat pasta, legumes, whole grains, etc. These are the foods that are very low in fat, no cholesterol, very low in sodium and high in energy and fiber. These foods contain the "good stuff" we need for good health and weight control.

NOTES

PIZZA SANDWICH

Per Serving:

Calories: 290   Sodium: 710 mg

Fat: 8 g   Fiber: 4.25 g

This dish is like a goulash - the vegetables and meat cook together. I like to prepare meals this way, then I don't have to cook vegetables as a side dish.

SICILIAN PASTA
Makes 6 servings

3

4 cups boiling water
3 cups WHOLE WHEAT PASTA

1/2 pound ground white turkey
1 medium onion, chopped
2 garlic cloves, minced
2 TB WHOLE WHEAT FLOUR
8 oz fresh mushrooms, coarsely chopped
1 large green pepper (use the seeds)
2 cans (14 1/2 oz) tomatoes
1/2 cup spaghetti sauce ((*Healthy Choice*)
2 TB Italian seasoning

The key to getting this meal to the table quickly is to put a pot of hot water on to boil right away. As soon as it boils, put in the pasta. You can use any kind of whole wheat pasta, but I like macaroni. While the pasta simmers for 10 minutes, do the following:

Brown the turkey with the onion and garlic; stir in the flour; chop the mushrooms and green pepper in your hands and add to the mixture; stir in the tomatoes, the spaghetti sauce and the Italian seasoning, and simmer.

You can either serve the sauce over the pasta, or combine the pasta and sauce. Serve it however you think your family will enjoy it best.

I like to have a piece of whole wheat bread with this meal.

NOTES

SICILIAN PASTA

Per Serving:

Calories: 300   *Sodium: 320 mg*

Fat: 2.5 g   *Fiber: 8.6 g*

Want a quick, easy, hearty, lowfat lunch? Try this one. Most all offices are equipped with a microwave, can opener, and a refrigerator, so you can take the fixin's to work with you. If you fix lunch at home for yourself or for your children, this one is a snap.

SPUDS & MORE   4
Makes 1 serving

1 medium potato
1 cup Beef Vegetable Soup *(Healthy Choice)*

Bake potato in the microwave until done. Put potato on a microwaveable plate, split in half, and mash it a bit. Top with the soup. Place back in the microwave and heat until the soup is warm. (Put the leftover soup in a container in the fridge to eat later.) What could be simpler?

Like most all soups, Healthy Choice is high in sodium, but when it is added to a potato (which has virtually no salt) the entire meal is low in sodium.

This can be a very good evening meal for the family. You just need to allow extra time for more potatoes to cook.

This is a very lowfat meal that is high in vitamins, minerals, fiber, and complex carbohydrates. The CCs (complex carbohydrates) are what give us energy for our muscles as well as for brain power.

I think you'll enjoy not only how good this meal tastes, but also how quick it is to fix. Just keep these two simple ingredients on hand, and you have a nutritious meal in no time.

FOOD FOR THOUGHT
What happens when we're driving down the road and we lift up on the accelerator? Our car slows down, doesn't it? The same thing happens to our body when we don't feed it. And what is our fuel? The energy foods. Keep your tank on full, using the "Fabulous 30" foods.

NOTES

SPUDS & MORE

Per Serving:

Calories: 350   Sodium: 435 mg

Fat: 1.2 g   Fiber: 5.6 g

This recipe is so quick to fix, and you don't have to cook a thing! Also, this is great to throw together in the morning before going to work, and then it's waiting on you. All you have to do is get out the plates!

QUICK MEXICAN SALAD   5
Makes 6 servings

1 can (15 oz) each
>   BLACK BEANS *(Ranch Style)*
>   CHILI HOT BEANS *(Bush's)*
>   GREAT NORTHERN BEANS *(Bush's)*
>   (drain all beans, but do not rinse)
1 large red bell pepper, chopped (use the seeds)
2/3 cup mild salsa *(Pace)*
1/2 cup chopped green onions
1 garlic clove, minced

4 oz shredded, low moisture, part skim mozzarella cheese

Mix the ingredients together - all but the cheese. Serve the shredded mozzarella on the side, and if you want cheese, sprinkle a very small amount on top. That's all! Enjoy!!

This is fantastic served with cornbread. If you don't want to go to the trouble of making cornbread, just serve Guiltless Gourmet Tortilla Chips or some whole grain crackers. Your family will love you for this one, & you'll like it because it's so simple and nutritious.

NOTE: If you need to watch your sodium intake, I would suggest rinsing the canned beans and using just a small amount of salsa. If you want to change this recipe the next time you fix it, try turkey or chicken instead of the cheese. The deli-thin pieces torn into bits is a good way to fix it.

FOOD FOR THOUGHT
We should always plan our meals around the energy foods. A minimum of 50% (more if active) of our food consumption should come from these foods. A minimum of 30% should come from neutral foods (fruits and vegetables) and not over 10% from the fat foods.

NOTES

QUICK MEXICAN SALAD

Per Serving:

Calories: 260   Sodium: 825 mg

Fat: 4.3 g   Fiber: 11 g

Yes, Mexicans eat pasta too. I know many of you like Mexican food but are concerned about all the fat that is in it. These Mexican recipes are excellent and do not have the fat of traditional Mexican dishes.

Mexican dishes normally contain Monterey Jack or cheddar cheese. Both of these cheeses are extremely high in fat. This is why I have chosen to use low moisture, part skim mozzarella cheese. Who says we can't change the cheese around a little?

As a side dish, the following recipe doesn't have cheese, but if we want a complete meal, we need to add some cheese, meat, or a complimentary plant food such as legumes. Since most of us are interested in quick complete meals, that is what this recipe will be.

MEXICAN PASTA   6
Makes 4 servings

3 cups boiling water
2 cups WHOLE WHEAT PASTA

1 can (14 1/2 oz) tomatoes with jalapeños
1 garlic clove, minced
4 ounces shredded, low moisture, part skim
    mozzarella cheese

SERVE WITH THIS MEAL:
Fresh or frozen steamed vegetables such as:
Broccoli, carrots, cauliflower, green pepper, etc.

Cook the pasta (use whatever shape your family likes) in boiling water for 10 minutes. After it is cooked, drain it and then add the tomatoes and garlic. Top with the cheese.

While the pasta cooks, heat the veggies for just a few minutes and serve them as is - no butter. If you're used to the fatty taste, this new taste will be a surprise to you, but you will grow to enjoy the "real" taste of the vegetables.

As you can see, this takes less than 15 minutes to get to the table. Also, these are foods that you can keep on hand to throw together at the last minutes. Enjoy!

NOTES

MEXICAN PASTA

Per Serving:

Calories: 285	*Sodium: 345 mg*
Fat: 6 g	*Fiber: 6.8 g*

I'll have to admit, lowfat Mexican meals rate quite high on my want list. This one, with a bit of Southwest flavor, takes less than 15 minutes to get to the table and tastes wonderful. Can't beat a meal like this!

THE ALBUQUERQUE SPECIAL 7
Makes 4 large servings

14 1/2 oz chicken broth *(Swanson 1/3 Less Sodium)*
2 cups QUICK COOKING BROWN RICE *(Uncle Ben's)*

2 tsp. sunflower oil
1 garlic clove, minced
1 medium onion, chopped
2 small zucchini, thinly sliced

2 cans (14 1/2 oz) tomatoes
1 can (4 oz) chopped green chilies *(Old El Paso)*

2 oz shredded, low moisture, part skim mozzarella cheese

Bring broth to boil; add rice. Cover and simmer on lowest heat 8 to 10 minutes.

While the rice cooks, saute garlic and onion in a large skillet; add zucchini and stir. Add tomatoes and green chilies. Heat till bubbly. That's all there is to it!

Serve the zucchini mixture on top of the rice, and then top each serving with just a light sprinkle of shredded mozzarella cheese. (If you want a vegetarian meal, omit the cheese.)

NOTES: If the zucchini mixture is too juicy for you, drain off a bit of the juice. Save it to drink chilled. It's very tasty!

If you use whole canned tomatoes, cut them into chunks while they're simmering in the skillet.

If you need a low sodium dish, use no-salt canned tomatoes. There are some very good choices on the market.

Remember, to save time, chop the onion and slice the zucchini in your hands, and just let them fall into the skillet.

Your family will love you for this meal! If there is any left over, take it to work with you for lunch. (The next time you make this meal, you may want to double the recipe so there will be enough for two meals.)

NOTES

THE ALBUQUERQUE SPECIAL

Per Serving:

Calories: 315   Sodium: 760 mg

Fat: 6.4 g   Fiber: 4.6 g

Are you in the mood for a cool meal - one that requires no cooking, is very low in fat, takes just a few minutes to prepare and tastes fantastic? Then write down these ingredients NOW and pick them up at your store today! You're familiar with 'A Hole in One'? Well, this is 'A Meal in One'.

VEGETABLE MEDLEY   8
Makes 5 servings

2 cups frozen PEAS
2 cups frozen CORN

2 cups chopped tomatoes
1 cup broccoli florets
1 cup sliced, fresh mushrooms
2 ribs celery, sliced
1/2 cup chopped onion

Shredded, low moisture, part skim mozzarella cheese
(optional)

FAT FREE ITALIAN DRESSING

1 1/4 cups water
2 TB vinegar
1 garlic clove, minced
1 packet Italian Fat Free Dressing Mix *(Good Seasons)*

To thaw the corn and peas, combine them in a large microwaveable dish and microwave on high for 4 minutes. Prepare the remaining vegetables and add to the corn and peas.

Put all the dressing ingredients in a container with a tight lid, and shake vigorously till mixed. Add to vegetable mixture and stir. That's it! Enjoy!

This is a complete meal in itself - the peas and corn make a complete protein - but if you want to add a small sprinkling of shredded mozzarella, go ahead. This will give the meal some vitamin B12 - and a small amount of fat.

Try different veggies; red or green bell pepper, zucchini and/or yellow squash, cucumbers, green onion, cauliflower, etc. (I always use tomatoes as they just 'make' this dish.)

NOTES

VEGETABLE MEDLEY

Per Serving (without cheese):

Calories: 130   *Sodium: 65 mg*

Fat: .7 g   *Fiber: 4.5 g*

There must be something wrong - this just tastes too good to be lowfat, nutritious and quick! This is 'Chip & Dip' made into a complete meal. When we think of chips and dip, we automatically think of high fat. Not so in this case. There are some tortilla chips on the market that are made without fat. Of course they're not going to taste like the grease laden varieties - but they are very tasty.

A MEXICAN QUICKIE 9
Makes 1 serving

1 serving TORTILLA CHIPS, about 20 *(Guiltless Gourmet)*
1/2 cup REFRIED BEANS *(Rosarita, No Fat)*
4 TB Picante sauce *(Pace)*

VEGGIES:
Carrot sticks and cauliflower florets

It takes virtually no effort to get this meal together. Just set the bag of chips on the table, open a can of refried beans, put a jar of picante sauce on the table, wash the veggies, and eat!

For all of us Mexican food lovers, this is truly heaven- sent. Besides being so quick and tasting so fabulous, this is very nutritious. It is brimming with energy, with the chips and beans, then the veggies round it out for a complete meal. (Use whatever veggies you like.) If you want to add some grated cheese for vitamin B12, go right ahead. Just be sure that it is a light sprinkling of cheese. (Don't ruin an excellent meal with fat.) Low moisture, part skim mozzarella is a good choice.
Guiltless Gourmet Chips are an excellent source of absorbable calcium because they are processed with lime.
If your store does not carry Guiltless Gourmet, ask for them to be ordered.

FOOD FOR THOUGHT
Diets make you fat. They also make you miserable!

NOTES

A MEXICAN QUICKIE

Per Serving:

Calories: 250   Sodium: 1170 mg

Fat: 1 g   Fiber: 8 g

This lowfat meal is a breeze to throw together. Even with preparing the chicken breasts yourself, this meal takes less than 15 minutes to get on the table! Notice that the name is "Hot & Spicy"? The name is accurate. It is hot!

HOT & SPICY CHICKEN   **10**
Makes 4 servings

3 1/4 cups boiling water
3 cups QUICK COOKING BROWN RICE *(Uncle Ben's)*

2 tsp. sunflower oil
2 boneless chicken breast halves, thinly sliced
2 garlic cloves, minced
1 medium onion, chopped
2 celery ribs, sliced
1 large green bell pepper, chopped (use the seeds)
4 oz fresh mushrooms, sliced
2 medium tomatoes, chopped

SAUCE:
3/4 cup cold water
1 TB soy sauce
1 pkg. Kung Pao Chicken, Seasoning Mix *(S&B)*

Simmer rice in the boiling water for 10 minutes. (Do not add butter or salt to the water.)

While the rice simmers, sauté chicken in oil in a large skillet until there is no pink showing. Add remaining vegetables, and simmer for just a couple minutes.

While this is simmering, stir together the sauce mixture. (I like to use a 2 cup measuring cup.) Stir the sauce into the simmering chicken & veggies. Heat till bubbly.

Serve this mixture on top of the brown rice. Enjoy!

This dish is great for those who like hot & spicy food, but it may be too hot for those who like blander food. For a less spicy sauce, use only part of the Kung Pao packet.

NOTE: You might want to double this recipe to have some left over to freeze in individual packages. Now, you will have your own frozen dinners to pop in the microwave.

NOTES

HOT & SPICY CHICKEN

Per Serving:

Calories: 445   Sodium: 805 mg

Fat: 6.5 g   Fiber: 7 g

I like this dish because I dirty only one pot! (Who likes to wash dishes?) This takes less than 15 minutes to fix, it is packed with nutrients; complex carbohydrates, vitamins, minerals, fiber, etc. - AND, it is very low in fat.

EGGPLANT WITH TURKEY   11
Makes 8 servings

1 tsp. sunflower oil
1 medium onion, chopped
2 garlic cloves, minced
1 medium green bell pepper, chopped (use the seeds)
1 can (15 oz) Italian Tomato Sauce *(Hunt's)*
2 cans (14 1/2 oz each) chicken broth
      (Swanson, 1/3 Less Sodium)
1 pound eggplant, diced but not peeled
1 pound thinly sliced, cooked turkey or chicken torn
      into bits (Deli meat is great to use.)
2 1/2 cups QUICK COOKING BROWN RICE
      (Uncle Ben's)
2 TB Italian Seasoning
Pepper to taste

Sauté onion & garlic in hot oil. Add remaining ingredients. Heat to boiling, then turn to lowest heat, cover and simmer for 10 minutes. That's all!
Serve with whole wheat bread, if you'd like.
If you want a low salt meal, use a "no salt" tomato sauce, and use a bit more Italian seasoning.
This truly is a yummy meal, and there should be enough left over to heat up for lunch tomorrow. Enjoy!

FOOD FOR THOUGHT
Throw the bathrooms scales away! Let's not play mental games with ourselves. With those darned scales, we get excited when we lose five pounds, even though it may be just water. Then we get depressed when we gain five pounds, even though it may be all muscle acquired through our new exercise program.

NOTES

EGGPLANT WITH TURKEY

Per Serving:

Calories: 220   *Sodium: 1170 mg*

Fat: 2.5 g   *Fiber: 3.4 g*

This recipe takes less than 15 minutes to get to the table and tastes fantastic!

SIMPLY SOUTHWEST   12
Makes 4 large servings

1 can (14 1/2 oz) chicken broth
    (Swanson, 1/3 Less Sodium)
2 1/4 cups QUICK COOKING BROWN RICE
    (Uncle Ben's)

2 tsp. sunflower oil
1 medium onion, chopped
2 garlic cloves, minced

2 cups diced cooked turkey *(Louis Rich)*
2 cups (2 small) thinly sliced zucchini
1 medium red bell pepper, chopped (use the seeds)
1 tsp. ground cumin
1/2 cup picante sauce *(Pace)*

Whole wheat bread *(optional, but recommended)*

Bring broth to boil; add rice. Cover and simmer on lowest heat 8 to 10 minutes. While it simmers, saute onion & garlic in the oil. Add remaining ingredients to the onion/garlic mixture, and cook for just a very few minutes - just till the vegetables are tender-crisp. Serve the turkey mixture on top of the rice. (I may have a slice of Earth Grain whole wheat bread with this meal.)

This dish can be made extra hot & spicy by the kind of picante sauce you use. Use 'hot' picante sauce for an extra hot dish, or use 'mild' sauce for just a bit of spicy flavor.

Green bell pepper can be substituted for red, but the red pepper makes this a beautiful dish, plus it 'ups' the beta carotene a tremendous amount.

Also, you can use leftover cooked chicken or turkey. I like to bake a small turkey just to have meat available for dishes like this.

For variety, experiment with different vegetables the next time you make this dish. A suggestion; try thin carrot slices and bite size pieces of cauliflower. Be creative.

This dish is very low in fat - and it tastes great! Enjoy.

NOTES

Want a fun meal that's super quick to fix and very nutritious - plus low in fat? Then this one's for you.

VEGGIE SPUD
Makes 1 serving

13

1 medium BAKING POTATO

1 tsp. sunflower oil
1 small garlic clove, minced
2 green onions (use entire onion)
1 cup frozen vegetables (California Style)

1/4 cup shredded, low moisture, part skim
   mozzarella cheese

Put the potato in the microwave to cook. (Of course, scrub and puncture it.) Sauté veggies in the oil just until they're tender-crisp. After the potato is cooked, cut it in half and mash a bit with a fork. Pour the veggies over the potato, and top with the shredded cheese.

If you want your potato to have more moisture, just add a little plain nonfat yogurt when you mash the potato. This takes the place of high fat sour cream.

This is one of the meals I like to throw together when I'm in a hurry. I nearly always have these ingredients on hand for those times when I haven't planned ahead.

If you want more servings, just increase everything as needed.

FOOD FOR THOUGHT
When humans are given complete freedom of choice, we tend to make choices based solely on "immediate" pleasures without any thought for the consequences of tomorrow. In the writings of W.C. Fields, he once described this human weakness in this way, "Once during the prohibition, I was forced to live for days on nothing but food and water."

NOTES

VEGGIE SPUD

Per Serving:

Calories: 460   Sodium: 250 mg

Fat: 5 g   Fiber: 10 g

Many people like taboli (tabbouleh) but the high fat content keeps many of us away from it. The following version is packed with energy and is low in fat while it retains all the scrumptious flavor of the high fat variety.

TABOLI SALAD   **14**
Makes 15, one cup servings

9 cups very hot tap water
3 cups (1 pound) TABOLI WHEAT (bulgur)

5 large tomatoes
2 bunches green onions (use entire onion)
1 bunch fresh parsley

DRESSING:
1/3 cup sunflower oil
1/3 cup lemon juice *(fresh, or frozen Minute Maid)*
3 garlic cloves, minced
1 tsp. salt

Soak wheat in the hot water for 15 minutes. While it's soaking, chop the tomatoes, onions, and parsley. (Be sure to use a big bowl, because this makes a lot!) Mix the dressing ingredients in a glass measuring cup. After the wheat has soaked, drain it well, then mix all ingredients together in the big bowl. If you want a tangier taste, add more lemon juice.

The energy in this meal comes from the taboli wheat (bulgur). Bulgur is very similar in energy to other whole grains, only with a little different flavor. Some people really get "hooked" on this dish. See what you think. (This is a vegetarian dish. To get vitamin B12, just add some animal food; nonfat yogurt, lowfat cottage cheese, or low moisture, part skim mozzarella cheese.)

If you want to use a food processor to chop your veggies, go right ahead. Even though I have one, I like to chop food in my hands.

I know this recipe makes a lot of taboli salad, but this dish gets better (the flavors mix) when it sets in the refrigerator. Also, it is great to have leftovers to take to work. Enjoy!

NOTES

TABOLI SALAD

Per Serving:

Calories: 155   Sodium: 170 mg

Fat: 6.8 g   Fiber: 4.6 g

This definitely is a "stay with you" meal. It's quick too - only 15 minutes, and it's on the table!

QUICK BARLEY & TUNA PILAF **15**
Makes 5 servings

1/2 cup chopped onion
2 garlic cloves, minced
2 cans (14 1/2 oz) chicken broth
     (Swanson, 1/3 Less Sodium)
1 box (11 oz) QUICK BARLEY *(Quaker)*
2 cups FROZEN PEAS
1 medium red bell pepper, chopped (use the seeds)
1 can (6 1/2 oz) water pack tuna, drained
Pepper to taste

In a large skillet, heat a small amount of chicken broth (about 1/4 cup). Saute onion & garlic in the broth. Add remaining broth & heat to boiling. Add remaining ingredients; reduce heat, cover & simmer for 10 minutes. That's it!!

This makes a very pretty meal because of the red pepper and the green peas. I would serve whole wheat bread with this meal, as well as carrot sticks.

If you feel that you must have more salt, add just a little. The chicken broth and the tuna both contain plenty of sodium. For those of you who need a very low sodium meal, use salt free tuna.

This makes a lot of pilaf, which is great to have for leftovers. Take some to work with you for lunch, or have the leftovers for dinner in a couple days. Enjoy!

FOOD FOR THOUGHT

We must stay motivated; we must stay informed; we must know what the food industry is going to be trying to serve us at our next meal. Together, we will win! I stay motivated by writing "The Companion". You stay motivated by reading "The Companion". To order "The Companion", see pages 111 and 117.

NOTES

QUICK BARLEY & TUNA PILAF

Per Serving:

Calories: 305   Sodium: 575 mg

Fat: 1.8 g   Fiber: 8.7 g

When the weather is cold, our thoughts automatically turn to soups and stews, but crock pot soups and stews are great anytime of the year Crock pot meals are so easy to throw together in a matter of minutes and they'll be waiting on us in the evening. This meal takes only 7 minutes to toss in the pot before we leave for work in the morning And this meal is very low in fat and high in energy.

ITALIAN SOUP 16
Makes 15, one cup servings

6 medium carrots*
1 large onion
2 garlic cloves
3 celery ribs
3 cans (16 oz) tomatoes *(Del Monte Italian Stewed)*
5 cups hot water
1 TB Italian Seasoning
Pepper to taste

2 cups QUICK COOKING BROWN RICE

Low moisture, part skim mozzarella cheese (optional)

Scrub the carrots, leave whole and put in bottom of crock pot - put largest carrots on the very bottom. Slice the onion as you would an apple, cut celery in bite-size pieces; add the canned tomatoes, hot water, seasoning and pepper. Let cook on low heat 10-12 hours.

As soon as you get home, turn the heat to high, and add the brown rice. Cover and cook for 15 minutes. Do not lift the lid before 15 minutes.

This is a vegetarian meal with no vitamin B12. Every meal doesn't have to heave B12, but if you want, serve thin slices of mozzarella cheese on whole grain crackers to get B12 in this meal.

*When carrots are left whole, they have a much better flavor (and it saves time to leave them whole).

NOTES

ITALIAN SOUP

Per Serving (without cheese):

Calories: 90   *Sodium: 410 mg*

Fat: .5 g   *Fiber: 3.7 g*

What do you do with leftover turkey? Why not make chili with it?

A few years ago, we thought that chili should be made only with ground beef or ground pork. Lately we have discovered that chili tastes pretty good made with ground turkey. In fact, many people can't tell the difference in these chilies.

Have you tried chili made with cooked turkey? Talk about quick & easy! This goes together in a very few minutes. The recipe below takes about 10 minutes. This is my kind of meal!!

SPEEDY CHILI 17
Makes 6, one cup servings

1 tsp. sunflower oil
1 cup chopped onion
1 minced garlic clove

1 cup cooked turkey, cut in small pieces
2 cans (16 oz) CHILI HOT BEANS *(Bush's)*
1 can (14 1/2 oz) tomatoes
1/2 package Chili Seasoning Mix *(Williams)*

Saute onion and garlic in the oil. Add remaining ingredients, and heat till bubbly. That's all!!

EAT WITH THIS: Whole grain crackers, carrot sticks & cauliflower florets.

Now, if you're watching your sodium intake, you will want to purchase "No Salt" tomatoes. You will also want to rinse the chili beans. Most all chili seasoning mixes are loaded with salt, but Williams isn't. It is salt free.

Since this recipe makes only 6 cups, I suggest doubling or tripling the recipe. This freezes well, thus making it very handy to pop in the microwave after a busy day. Also, it is convenient to freeze individual servings to take to work with you.

Many chilies are quite high in fat. Rest assured, this one is extremely low. When your friends ask how you can eat chili and not gain weight, just sorta smile and walk on! (On second thought, tell them about *15 MINUTE LOWFAT MEALS!)*

NOTES

SPEEDY CHILI

Per Serving:

Calories: 195   *Sodium: 680 mg*

Fat: 2.7 g   *Fiber: 8 g*

This recipe doesn't sound very original, but it is. It is very low in fat. Most all Tuna Noodle Casserole recipes I know about call for sour cream. Here, we use nonfat yogurt instead of sour cream. This is a one-dish meal. (We dirty two pans to fix it, but everything we need for a complete meal is combined into one dish.) This casserole takes less than 15 minutes to get to the table!

TUNE NOODLE CASSEROLE 18
Makes 5 large servings

4 cups boiling water
3 cups WHOLE WHEAT NOODLES

1 medium onion, chopped
1 tsp. sunflower oil
1 cup plain nonfat yogurt
2 tsp. Worcestershire Sauce
1 can (6 1/2 oz) water packed tuna*
3 cups frozen mixed vegetables**
Pepper to taste

Cook noodles in boiling water for 8 minutes. While they're cooking, brown the onion in oil. Add the remaining ingredients and cook until hot - about 5 minutes. Drain the noodles, then combine everything into one dish. Serve with whole wheat bread.

This is an excellent one-dish, high energy casserole that we really enjoy. See what you think!

*Mackerel or salmon can be substituted for the tuna. Use the bones for more calcium.

**Choose mixed vegetables your family enjoys such as cauliflower, carrots, and green beans. You may certainly use fresh veggies instead of frozen.

FOOD FOR THOUGHT
Without fiber in our foods, it's difficult to know when we're full. We just keep right on eating.

NOTES

TUNA NOODLE CASSEROLE

Per Serving:

Calories: 220   *Sodium: 225 mg*

Fat: 2.25 g   *Fiber: 6.3 g*

Pasta salads are great anytime, but a cold pasta salad is particularly inviting in summertime. This very tasty salad takes less than 15 minutes to get to the table and there is only one pan to wash!

MINESTRONE SALAD   19
Makes 8, one cup servings

3 cups boiling water
2 cups WHOLE WHEAT PASTA

2 cans (15 oz) BLACK BEANS, rinsed (*Ranch Style*)
2 cans (14 oz) Italian stewed tomatoes
1 bunch green onions, chopped (use entire onion)
1 garlic clove, minced
Pepper to taste

Shredded, low moisture, part skim mozzarella (optional)

Cook pasta in boiling water for 10 minutes. (I like to use whole wheat macaroni.) While it is cooking, prepare remaining ingredients and put in a serving bowl. Add the drained pasta & stir. That's all! Top with a small amount of shredded mozzarella if you want.

This dish is a complete protein without the cheese. The black beans, a legume, and the pasta, a grain, make this a complete protein - however, it has no vitamin B12. The cheese provides B12 and more flavor - and some fat.

This is a great dish to fix when you get home in the evening, or fix it early in the morning so it will be ready in the evening when you walk in the house. (This salad is good hot or cold.) Many of us are busy with childrens' ball games, dance lessons, etc. in the evenings, and this quick-to-fix meal will be a godsend for those busy days. Do give this a try.

FOOD FOR THOUGHT
The diet industry's favorite slogan: "We never cure them. We never kill them. But they just keep coming back and spending more and more money."

83

NOTES

MINESTRONE SALAD

Per Serving (without cheese):

Calories: 215   Sodium: 720 mg

Fat: .5 g   Fiber: 10 g

Did you know that Americans consume more than 10 billion bowls of soup each year? In the month of January, we buy 57 million gallons of soup. This averages 100 cans of condensed soup every second of every day in January!

Soup is so convenient to pack in a lunch pail or take to the office. Soup can come in a can, a box, a microwaveable cup, a cellophane bag, and it even comes frozen. Unfortunately sodium and fat are high in many soups. However, we can make our own. This potato soup is a favorite with my family and takes only 15 minutes to get to the table.

POTATO SOUP   **20**
Makes 9, one cup servings

1 tsp. sunflower oil
1 medium onion, chopped
3 garlic cloves, minced
2 celery ribs, sliced
2 cans (14 1/2 oz) chicken broth
    (Swanson, 1/3 Less Sodium)
3 medium POTATOES, cut in _small_ pieces

2 cups skim milk*
1 TB dried parsley flakes (or 1/3 cup fresh)
Pepper to taste

Sauté onion in oil; add ingredients through potatoes and heat to boiling. Simmer 10 minutes on medium-high heat, uncovered. Add remaining ingredients and heat till mixture begins to boil. Serve in soup bowls or mugs.

Serve with whole wheat crackers or whole wheat pretzels and raw veggies such as carrot sticks, green pepper slices, cauliflower, etc.

* If you have a problem with milk, use lowfat Acidophilus or lowfat Dairy Ease.

An old Yiddish saying: "Troubles are easier to take with soup than without."

An old Spanish proverb: "Of soup and love, the first is best."

A quote from Jeff Smith, The Frugal Gourmet: "I cannot put into words the comfort I find in soup. Soup is like wine - it should be enjoyed with others."

NOTES

POTATO SOUP

Per Serving:

Calories: 120   Sodium: 290 mg

Fat: .6 g   Fiber: 1.7 g

Many times people have asked me how to cook a pot of beans if ham isn't used for flavoring. (The reason we choose not to use cured ham is that it contained cancer-causing nitrites and is high in fat.)

My family just loves the flavor and zip of these beans. If you want to use some meat (animal flesh) just add a couple of skinned chicken breasts or a few skinned thighs.

PEPPY PINTOS   **21**
Makes 11, one cup servings

3 1/2 cups dried PINTO BEANS
7 cups hot water
1 medium onion, chopped
1 can (7 oz) chopped green chilies
4 garlic cloves, minced
1 1/2 TB chili powder
1 tsp. salt (optional)

Wash pintos thoroughly (looking for small stones). Add all ingredients to a crock pot. Stir and cook on low heat 12 hours or longer.

EAT WITH THIS:
Corn bread
Carrot sticks
Cauliflower florets

If you don't want to take the time to make corn bread, just eat whole grain crackers or Guiltless Gourmet Tortilla Chips.

It's a real treat to walk in the house on a cold blustery evening after work and smell a pot of beans ready to eat. I hope you like this version of cooked pintos as much as we do.

FOOD FOR THOUGHT
We say we don't have the energy to exercise. That's understandable. It is difficult to have energy when we don't eat the energy foods.

NOTES

PEPPY PINTOS

Per Serving (includes salt):

Calories: 70   Sodium: 310 mg

Fat: .28 g   Fiber: 3.5 g

So many people love this dish! It's quick to fix, it's very tasty, very low in fat, and it's filled with energy.

LAREDO POTATO 22
Makes 1 serving

1 medium POTATO
1/4 cup CHILI HOT BEANS *(Bush's)*
1/2 tomato, chopped
2 TB chopped green onion
1/2 oz shredded, low moisture, part skim
      mozzarella cheese

2 TB Salsa *(Pace)*

Bake potato in microwave 4 minutes - or till done; split and mash a bit. Top with the beans. Heat in microwave. Top with tomato, onion, and cheese. Now add salsa for great Mexican flavor.

EAT WITH THIS:
1 small carrot
1/2 medium green pepper

This is soooooooo quick and easy! And it's packed with gobs of energy and is very lowfat. Keep the ingredients on hand, and you'll always have a tasty meal available.

I strongly recommend low moisture, part skim mozzarella cheese as it is lower in fat, cholesterol and sodium than other natural cheeses.

FOOD FOR THOUGHT
God gave us two ends. One to sit on and one to think with. Health depends upon which one we use most. Heads we win. Tails we lose.

89

NOTES

LAREDO POTATO

Per Serving:

Calories: 320   Sodium: 560 mg

Fat: 3 g   Fiber: 9.5 g

One of the reasons we hardly ever see overweight, native, Oriental people is because of the way they eat. If we eat meals like this one on a regular basis, people will say the same about us!

ORIENTAL BEEF & VEGETABLE STIR-FRY 23
Makes 6 servings

2 1/4 cups boiling water
2 cups QUICK COOKING BROWN RICE *(Uncle Ben's)*

1 pound *lean* beef (loins are best)
1 tsp. sunflower oil
2 cups broccoli florets
2 cups chunked, fresh mushrooms
1 medium red bell pepper, chopped (use the seeds)

1 TB cornstarch
1 TB soy sauce
3/4 cup cold water

Add rice to the boiling water; cover and simmer on lowest heat for 10 minutes. While the rice cooks, trim all fat from meat & slice thinly. In a large skillet, brown meat in hot oil; add vegetables and stir. Mix cornstarch, soy sauce and water; add to skillet, stir and cover. Reduce heat and cook until sauce thickens - maybe one minute. Serve over the rice.

You may certainly use regular brown rice. In fact, I like the flavor and texture of regular brown rice better than quick cooking. It just takes longer to cook. When you're not in a hurry, use the regular rice - brown, that is - and see what you think.
This is a beautiful, nutritious, lowfat and high energy meal. It is one of my favorite meals to serve to dinner guests.

FOOD FOR THOUGHT
95% of all diets fail - which makes dieters failures. Kinda' hard to have a good, positive attitude as a failure!

NOTES

ORIENTAL BEEF & VEGETABLE STIR-FRY

Per Serving:

Calories: 315   Sodium: 295 mg

Fat: 9 g   Fiber: 3.3 g

I get many requests for recipes that do not contain meat, yet still provide complete protein. This recipe is one of my favorites. It is a very high energy meal, very lowfat, high in fiber, and it's quick to fix.

VEGETARIAN CHILI   24
Makes 8, one cup servings

1 tsp. sunflower oil
1/2 cup chopped onion
2 garlic cloves, minced
2 cups QUICK COOKING BROWN RICE (Uncle Ben's)
2 cans (14 1/2 oz) tomatoes
2 cans (16 oz) CHILI HOT BEANS (Bush's)
1/2 package chili seasoning mix (Williams)

Sauté onion & garlic in oil; add remaining ingredients. Heat to boiling, then reduce heat; cover & simmer for 10 minutes. (If you want a thinner chili, just add some water. If you like a spicier chili, add more seasoning mix.)

If you want to top your chili with shredded cheddar, use only a very small amount - just enough for flavor.

EAT WITH THIS:
   WHOLE GRAIN CRACKERS or
   WHOLE GRAIN CORN BREAD
   Carrot sticks
   Raw cauliflower, or cabbage or broccoli
(Use whatever raw veggies your family likes.)   Enjoy!

FOOD FOR THOUGHT
75% of the products on our grocery shelves are absolutely worthless to us. (Maybe more in some stores!) How should we shop? We should find the "Fabulous 30" foods - put them in our cart, then spend the rest of our time deciding which fruits and vegetables look the best, and put them in our cart. Now, what should we do? Go home and enjoy eating and eating - without guilt - for a change!

NOTES

VEGETARIAN CHILI

Per Serving:

Calories: 225   Sodium: 595 mg

Fat: 2.2 g   Fiber: 7 g

Many people enjoy muffins. They are a grab-and-run food, and they make great snacks. They can also be health hazards because many 'store muffins' are made with nutrient deficient flour, and they're high in fat and sugar. These muffins are healthful. They're made with whole wheat flour and no sugar.

APPLESAUCE MUFFINS 25
Makes 36 mini muffins

2 cups WHOLE WHEAT FLOUR
     (or whole wheat pastry flour)
1 TB baking powder *(Rumford)*
1 tsp. baking soda
1/2 tsp. nutmeg
1/2 tsp. cinnamon
1 cup raisins
1/2 cup chopped pecans

1 1/2 cups unsweetened applesauce
1 egg

Heat oven to 375º.

Put all dry ingredients in a large bowl, making sure there are no lumps in the baking soda, and stir until the ingredients are mixed well. Make a well in the center of the mixture; add applesauce and egg. Stir applesauce and egg together until the egg is mixed in, then blend dry ingredients into the applesauce/ egg mixture. Stir just until moistened. (By mixing the ingredients this way, you dirty only one bowl!)

Fill lightly greased mini muffin cups 2/3 full. Bake 12-15 minutes.

FOOD FOR THOUGHT

We say it's awfully hard to resist temptation for those rich, fat-filled foods. Yes, I know. Do I ever know!! But I'll guarantee one thing, it's a lot easier to resist them when you're full than when you're on some crazy, calorie-counting diet. Just remember our philosophy - "Never Go Hungry."

NOTES

APPLESAUCE MUFFINS

Per Serving (1 mini muffin):

Calories: 55   *Sodium: 70 mg*

Fat: 1.4 g   *Fiber: 1.6 g*

What a simple meal to fix! Kids love macaroni & cheese, but nearly all boxed brands are made with nutrient deficient, highly processed pasta and contain artificial color. So - make your own in the same length of time it takes to make it from a box. Of course, yours will be a lot more healthful and won't add weight to the waistline!

MACARONI & CHEESE, ITALIAN STYLE   26
Makes 6, one cup servings

3 cups boiling water
2 cups WHOLE WHEAT MACARONI

1 cup spaghetti sauce *(Healthy Choice)*
2 garlic cloves, minced
2/3 cup fresh parsley (or 2 TB dried)

Low moisture, part skim mozzarella, shredded

Boil macaroni 8 minutes; drain. Put back into saucepan; add spaghetti sauce, garlic and parsley. Heat through and serve. Top each serving with 1/4 cup shredded mozzarella.

EAT WITH THIS:
    A variety of veggies raw or steamed, such as:
    Broccoli, cauliflower, carrots, green or red pepper.

The whole wheat pasta is packed with energy that kids - moms & dads too - need. Since we use such a small portion of cheese, this dish is lowfat. These ingredients are easy to keep on hand, and you can throw this meal together in nothing flat!

FOOD FOR THOUGHT
Recipe for aging:
    1. Loss of energy   3. Muscle decline
    2. Inactivity   4. Weight gain

NOTES

MACARONI & CHEESE ITALIAN STYLE

Per Serving (with cheese):

Calories: 225   *Sodium: 310 mg*

Fat: 5.7 g   *Fiber: 4.6 g*

This is a great dish to serve at home or take to a luncheon. It will probably be the only one like it there. I can assure you, you will be asked for the recipe!

BROWN RICE WALDORF SALAD 27
Makes 8, one cup servings

1 1/4 cups boiling water
1 cup QUICK COOKING BROWN RICE* *(Uncle Ben's)*

4 medium red apples, diced (do not peel)
2 TB lemon juice *(fresh, or frozen Minute Maid)*
2 TB apple juice concentrate
3 celery ribs, thinly sliced (1 1/2 cups)
1/2 cup chopped pecans
1/2 cup raisins
1 cup plain nonfat yogurt
1/2 tsp. cinnamon
1/4 tsp. nutmeg
1/4 tsp. allspice

Add rice to the boiling water. Turn to lowest heat; cover and simmer for 10 minutes. While it cooks, chop the apples in a serving bowl and add lemon juice to coat the apples. Add the remaining ingredients, including the cooked rice; stir well. Serve immediately or chill for later.

This is a wonderful meal that is filling, lowfat, nutritious, and packed with energy. This is one of our favorite meals, and I love it because I can fix it ahead and have it waiting in the fridge.

*Remember that you can use regular brown rice. In fact, I like the taste and texture of the regular rice, but it does take longer to cook. Use whichever you like.

FOOD FOR THOUGHT
"Real" food does not make us fat. Fats and highly processed foods make us fat.

NOTES

BROWN RICE WALDORF SALAD

Per Serving:

Calories: 190   *Sodium: 30 mg*

Fat: 5.6 g   *Fiber: 7.5 g*

This is a very quick meal that has a unique flavor because of the cabbage and tarragon. I love the flavor, and the dish is so colorful.

TARRAGON TURKEY **28**
Makes 4 servings

2 cans (14 1/2 oz) chicken broth
  (Swanson, 1/3 Less Sodium)
2 cups QUICK COOKING BROWN RICE *(Uncle Ben's)*

1/2 pound turkey breast, skinned & thinly sliced*
1 tsp. sunflower oil
1 garlic clove, minced
1/2 cup chopped onion
1 tsp. dried tarragon
2 cups shredded cabbage
1 cup chopped celery
1 medium red bell pepper, thinly sliced (use the seeds)

3/4 cup chicken broth *(Swanson, 1/3 Less Sodium)*
1 TB cornstarch

Heat chicken broth to boiling; add brown rice, reduce heat to simmer, cover and cook for 10 minutes.

While the rice cooks, brown the turkey on both sides in oil. Add the garlic, onion and tarragon. Stir and add cabbage, celery and red pepper. Mix broth and cornstarch; add to skillet and stir. Cover and simmer for 3-5 minutes. Stir and serve over the rice.

* You may certainly substitute chicken breast for the turkey. The flavor is similar, whichever you use.

This is a high energy, lowfat meal that is full of wonderful veggies packed with nutrients, flavor and color. You may substitute pimientos for the red pepper if you'd like. The red pepper has more nutrients and better flavor, but you may not be able to get them all during the year.

101

NOTES

TARRAGON TURKEY

Per Serving:

Calories: 340   Sodium: 760 mg

Fat: 4.7 g   Fiber: 5 g

THE "FABULOUS 30" RECIPES

I cannot describe to you the fantastic flavor this dish has - you just have to experience it for yourself! I call it "Chicken Surprise" because the flavor is unusual, but delicious.

CHICKEN SURPRISE   29
Makes 6 servings

14 1/2 oz chicken broth *(Swanson, 1/3 Less Sodium)*
2 cups QUICK COOKING BROWN RICE *(Uncle Ben's)*

1 can (15 oz) BLACK BEANS *(Ranch Style)*
1 cup bite-size, cooked chicken
1/2 cup plain, nonfat yogurt
1/3 cup sliced almonds
2 tsp. soy sauce
1/4 tsp. pepper
1/4 tsp. poultry seasoning

Heat broth to boiling; add rice, cover and simmer on lowest heat for 10 minutes.

While rice is cooking, combine remaining ingredients in a large serving dish. As soon as rice is done, add to serving dish. Mix well and serve immediately. That's all!

If you want to garnish this dish, some slices of tomato or red pepper would be great around the edges, along with some sprigs of parsley. Then sprinkle a few sliced almonds on top.

(You can use Louis Rich Oven Roasted Turkey Breast in place of cooked chicken. Or you can use leftover turkey.)

SUGGESTION: Make a big batch and freeze it for future meals.

Serve some steamed vegetables with this dish; such as broccoli and cauliflower or cabbage.

FOOD FOR THOUGHT
Definitions:
Old people food: Foods that make us fat and age prematurely.
Young people food: Foods that keep us trim, active and healthy.

NOTES

CHICKEN SURPRISE

Per Serving:

Calories: 260   Sodium: 590 mg

Fat: 4.7 g   Fiber: 5 g

All you chocolate lovers out there (which includes me) here's one for you!

CHOCOLATE MUFFINS   **30**
Makes 36 mini muffins

1 1/2 cups WHOLE WHEAT FLOUR
　　　or whole wheat pastry flour
6 TB cocoa
1 tsp. baking soda
1/2 tsp. baking powder *(Rumford)*
1/4 tsp. salt
1 cup raisins
1/2 cup chopped pecans

2 extra ripe bananas
1 egg
1/3 cup unsweetened applesauce
1/4 cup apple juice concentrate

Turn oven to 350°. In a large bowl, stir together flour, cocoa, soda, baking powder and salt. Add pecans and raisins. (Separate raisins if they're stuck together.)

In another bowl, mash the bananas; fold in egg, applesauce and apple juice concentrate.

Add liquid ingredients to dry ingredients and stir together until moistened.

Fill lightly greased mini muffin cups 2/3 full and bake 12-15 minutes.

These are very high energy, fiber filled muffins. Realize that these are not going to taste like the high fat, sugar filled, nutrient deficient muffins you find in most donut shops. The difference in these muffins and the others is just like the difference in white bread and whole wheat bread.

FOOD FOR THOUGHT
"At 40, I was starting to show my age, but I took my life back in control and now, 10 years later, I'm back to 30!"

NOTES

CHOCOLATE MUFFINS

Per Serving (1 mini muffin):

Calories: 55   *Sodium: 55 mg*

Fat: 1.5 g   *Fiber: 1.2 g*

EPILOGUE

The year was 1917, some seventy five years ago, when an educator by the name of Orville Swip made this statement while addressing a high school class in New England:

> "Every person who is not his own master is sure to have somebody or something else for his master sooner or later - usually sooner. Be boss of yourself, of your mind as well as your body, and success is assured."

I hope you enjoy these
quick, healthful meals
as much as my family does.

In Good Health,

Jayne

Jayne

INDEX

THE "FABULOUS 30" FOODS

THE "FABULOUS 30" RECIPES

ORDER FORM

"THE COMPANION"

☎ Telephone orders: Call TOLL FREE: 1(800) 580-1414.
Have your VISA, MasterCard, American Express, or
Discover Card ready.

▤ Fax orders: (405) 348-3741

✉ Postal orders: MEALS IN MINUTES,
P.O. Box 1828, Edmond, OK 73083-1828.
Tel: (405) 341-4545

Please send _____ year(s) subscription to "THE
COMPANION" under your money-back guarantee.

	Price:	1 year (10 issues)	$24.95
		2 years (20 issues)	$44.95
		3 years (30 issues)	$59.95

Name:_____

Address:_____

City:_____ State:_____ Zip:_____ - _____

Telephone:(_____)_____

Payment:
☐ Check ☐ Money Order for the total amount of
$_____which is enclosed.

Charge it to my:
☐ VISA ☐ MasterCard ☐ American Express ☐ Discover

Card number:_____
Name on card:_____
Exp. date:_____/_____

ORDER FORM

THE FOOD BIBLE

☎ Telephone orders: Call TOLL FREE: 1(800) 580-1414.
Have your VISA, MasterCard, American Express, or
Discover Card ready.

▤ Fax orders: (405) 348-3741

✉ Postal orders: MEALS IN MINUTES,
P.O. Box 1828, Edmond, OK 73083-1828.
Tel: (405) 341-4545

Please send _____ copie(s) of *THE FOOD BIBLE* under
your money-back guarantee.

Name:_____

Address:_____

City:_____ State:_____ Zip:_____ -_____

Telephone:(_____)_____

Price: $16.95 each. (Oklahoma residents please add $1.12
sales tax for a total of $18.07.)

Book Rate: $3.50 for the first book and 50 cents for each
additional book. (Book rate may take 1-2 weeks.)
First Class: $5.25 for the first book and $1.00 for each
additional book.

Payment: ☐ Check ☐ Money Order for the total amount
of $_____which is enclosed.

Charge it to my:
☐ VISA ☐ MasterCard ☐ American Express ☐ Discover

Card number:_____ Exp. date:____/____
Name on card:_____

114

ORDER FORM

15 MINUTE LOWFAT MEALS
A COOKBOOK FOR THE BUSY PERSON

☎ Telephone orders: Call TOLL FREE: 1(800) 580-1414.
Have your VISA, MasterCard, American Express, or
Discover Card ready.

▤ Fax orders: (405) 348-3741

✉ Postal orders: MEALS IN MINUTES,
P.O. Box 1828, Edmond, OK 73083-1828.
Tel: (405) 341-4545

Please send _____ copie(s) of *15 MINUTE LOWFAT
MEALS* under your money-back guarantee.

Name:_____

Address:_____

City:_____ State:_____ Zip:_____ -

Telephone:(_____)_____

Price: $10.95 each. (Oklahoma residents please add $.73
      sales tax for a total of $11.68.)

Shipping: $3.50 for the first book and $1.15 for each
      additional book.

Payment: ☐ Check ☐ Money Order for the total amount
of $_____which is enclosed.

Charge it to my:
☐ VISA   ☐ MasterCard   ☐ American Express   ☐ Discover

Card number:_____ Exp. date:___ / ___
Name on card:_____

ORDER FORM

"THE COMPANION"

☎ Telephone orders: Call TOLL FREE: 1(800) 580-1414. Have your VISA, MasterCard, American Express, or Discover Card ready.

▤ Fax orders: (405) 348-3741

✉ Postal orders: MEALS IN MINUTES, P.O. Box 1828, Edmond, OK 73083-1828. Tel: (405) 341-4545

Please send _____ year(s) subscription to "THE COMPANION" under your money-back guarantee.

Price:	1 year	(10 issues)	$24.95
	2 years	(20 issues)	$44.95
	3 years	(30 issues)	$59.95

Name:_____

Address:_____

City:_____ State:_____ Zip:_____ - _____

Telephone:(_____)_____

Payment:
□ Check □ Money Order for the total amount of $_____which is enclosed.

Charge it to my:
□ VISA □ MasterCard □ American Express □ Discover

Card number:_____
Name on card:_____
Exp. date:_____ /_____

ORDER FORM

THE FOOD BIBLE

☎ Telephone orders: Call TOLL FREE: 1(800) 580-1414.
Have your VISA, MasterCard, American Express, or
Discover Card ready.

▤ Fax orders: (405) 348-3741

✉ Postal orders: MEALS IN MINUTES,
P.O. Box 1828, Edmond, OK 73083-1828.
Tel: (405) 341-4545

Please send _____ copie(s) of *THE FOOD BIBLE* under
your money-back guarantee.

Name:_____

Address:_____

City:_____ State:_____ Zip:_____ - _____

Telephone:(_____)_____

Price: $16.95 each. (Oklahoma residents please add $1.12
sales tax for a total of $18.07.)

Book Rate: $3.50 for the first book and 50 cents for each
additional book. (Book rate may take 1-2 weeks.)
First Class: $5.25 for the first book and $1.00 for each
additional book.

Payment: ☐ Check ☐ Money Order for the total amount
of $_____which is enclosed.

Charge it to my:
☐ VISA ☐ MasterCard ☐ American Express ☐ Discover

Card number:_____ Exp. date:____ / ____
Name on card:_____

ORDER FORM

15 MINUTE LOWFAT MEALS
A COOKBOOK FOR THE BUSY PERSON

☎ Telephone orders: Call TOLL FREE: 1(800) 580-1414. Have your VISA, MasterCard, American Express, or Discover Card ready.

🖷 Fax orders: (405) 348-3741

✉ Postal orders: MEALS IN MINUTES, P.O. Box 1828, Edmond, OK 73083-1828. Tel: (405) 341-4545

Please send _____ copie(s) of *15 MINUTE LOWFAT MEALS* under your money-back guarantee.

Name:_____

Address:_____

City:_____ State:_____ Zip:_____ - _____

Telephone:(_____)_____

Price: $10.95 each. (Oklahoma residents please add $.73 sales tax for a total of $11.68.)

Shipping: $3.50 for the first book and $1.15 for each additional book.

Payment: ☐ Check ☐ Money Order for the total amount of $_____which is enclosed.

Charge it to my:
☐ VISA ☐ MasterCard ☐ American Express ☐ Discover

Card number:_____ Exp. date:____ / ____
Name on card:_____

ABOUT THE AUTHOR...
JAYNE BENKENDORF

CURRENT ACTIVITIES:

Owner - MEALS IN MINUTES
> A company dedicated to bringing the latest
> information on healthful food and healthy
> lifestyle to the public.

Author - *15 MINUTE LOWFAT MEALS*
> *A COOKBOOK FOR THE BUSY PERSON*
> Quick, healthful, lowfat meals for the person who doesn't have
> much time to spend in the kitchen.

> *The Food Bible*
> A book which lists food products free of harmful additives and
> preservatives. Each product is coded for its fat, sodium, sugar,
> and cholesterol content, and it is noted if the product is
> highly processed.

> *NEVER GO HUNGRY*®
> A complete program for natural and permanent weight control.
> This program consists of audio tapes and a book.

Editor & Publisher - "The Companion"
> A newsletter which keeps subscribers up to date on what is
> happening in the grocery store - the best foods and those to
> avoid. Special health issues are highlighted in "The
> Companion". Food preparation and meal planning ideas are
> included, direct from Jayne's kitchen.

Speaker - MEALS IN MINUTES
> Jayne travels nationally giving seminars to busy people demon-
> stating that you *can* get meals on the table in 15 minutes or
> less.

PAST ACTIVITIES:

Research - Oklahoma State University School of Veterinary Medicine

Registered Medical Technologist

Teaching cooking and meal planning

Certified Fitness Instructor